C. S. LEWIS AND FRIENDS

C. S. LEWIS AND FRIENDS

Faith and the power of imagination

Edited by
DAVID HEIN and
EDWARD HENDERSON

CASCADE *Books* · Eugene, Oregon

C. S. LEWIS AND FRIENDS

Published under license from Society for Promoting Christian Knowledge (SPCK), London, England.

Cascade Books
An Imprint of Wipf and Stock Publishers
199 W. 8th Ave., Suite 3
Eugene, OR 97401

www.wipfandstock.com

ISBN 13: 978-1-61097-791-3

Cataloging-in-Publication data:

Hein, David.

C. S. Lewis and Friends / David Hein and Edward Henderson.

x + 149 p. ; 22cm. —Includes bibliographical references and index.

ISBN 13: 978-1-61097-791-3

1. Lewis, C. S. (Clive Staples), 1898–1963. 2. Farrer, Austin, 1904–1968. 3. Sayers, Dorothy L. (Dorothy Leigh), 1893–1957. 4. William, Charles, 1886–1945. 5. Macauley, Dame Emilie Rose, 1881–1958. 6. Tolkien, J. R. R. (John Ronald Revel), 1892–1973. I. Henderson, Edward. II. Title.

PR6023. E926 C65 2011

Contents

Illustrations

Contributors

Charles Hefling is Associate Professor of Theology at Boston College. He is an expert on the work of both Austin Farrer and Charles Williams. In 1979 Cowley Publications brought out his *Jacob's Ladder: Theology and Spirituality in the Thought of Austin Farrer*. He has also contributed to two collections of essays about Farrer: *For God and Clarity: New Essays in Honor of Austin Farrer* (Pickwick, 1983) and *Captured by the Crucified: The Practical Theology of Austin Farrer* (T. & T. Clark/Continuum, 2004). In addition, Professor Hefling edited and wrote an introduction for *Charles Williams: Essential Writings in Spirituality and Theology* (Cowley, 1993).

David Hein is Professor of Religion and Philosophy at Hood College, Frederick, Maryland. He is co-editor with Edward Henderson of *Captured by the Crucified: The Practical Theology of Austin Farrer* (T. & T. Clark/Continuum, 2004) and the author of numerous books and articles. His essays on C. S. Lewis, Rose Macaulay, Austin Farrer and related subjects have appeared in *Theology*, the *Anglican Theological Review*, the *Sewanee Theological Review* and the *Anglican Digest*.

Edward Henderson is Professor of Philosophy and the Jaak Seynaeve Professor of Christian Studies at Louisiana State University, in Baton Rouge. He is co-editor of two collections of essays about Austin Farrer: with Brian Hebblethwaite, *Divine Action: Studies Inspired by the Philosophical Theology of Austin Farrer* (T. & T. Clark, 1990); and with David Hein, *Captured by the Crucified: The Practical Theology of Austin Farrer* (T. & T. Clark/Continuum, 2004). Inspired by Ralph Wood, he has recently taught a seminar called 'C. S. Lewis and the Oxford Christians', in which he covers Lewis, Tolkien, Williams, Sayers and Farrer.

Ann Loades, CBE, is Professor Emerita of Divinity in the University of Durham. Professor Loades has written on C. S. Lewis, Dorothy L. Sayers and Austin Farrer. She is co-editor of two books of essays about Farrer: *For God and Clarity* (Pickwick, 1983), which was the first collection of papers on Farrer to be published, and *Hermeneutics,* *the Bible and Literary Criticism* (St Martin's Press, 1992). She contributed to *Captured by the Crucified: The Practical Theology of Austin Farrer* (T. & T. Clark/Continuum, 2004); and, with Robert MacSwain, she edited *The Truth-Seeking Heart: Austin Farrer and His Writings* (Canterbury, 2006). Her interest in Dorothy L. Sayers led Professor Loades to select and introduce some of Sayers's spiritual writings for *Dorothy L. Sayers: Spiritual Writings* (Cowley, 1993) and to include a chapter on Sayers in her *Feminist Theology: Voices from the Past* (Polity, 2001).

Peter J. Schakel is the Emajean Cook Professor of English at Hope College, Holland, Michigan, and a prominent C. S. Lewis scholar. He is the author of *Reason and Imagination in C. S. Lewis: A Study of 'Till We Have Faces'* (Eerdmans, 1984), *Imagination and the Arts in C. S. Lewis: Journeying to Narnia and Other Worlds* (University of Missouri Press, 2002), *The Way into Narnia: A Reader's Guide* (Eerdmans, 2005), and *Is Your Lord Large Enough? How C. S. Lewis Expands Our View of God* (InterVarsity, 2008).

Ralph C. Wood is University Professor of Theology and Literature at Baylor University, Waco, Texas. Professor Wood's specialism has been the religious dimensions of such American novelists as William Faulkner, Flannery O'Connor, Walker Percy and John Updike; but some years ago he began teaching a course on C. S. Lewis and the Oxford Christians. This course covers Lewis, Tolkien, Sayers and Williams. It led to Wood's writing *The Gospel According to Tolkien: Visions of the Kingdom in Middle-earth* (Westminster John Knox, 2003) and many essays on Tolkien and Lewis.

Foreword

Although in our contemporary culture 'imagination' is generally used in a positive sense, this has by no means always been so. Indeed, we need only return to Scripture and liturgy to find more negative usages. Think, for instance, of the comment in Genesis that 'the imagination of man's heart is evil from his youth' (8.21 AV) or of Mary's *Magnificat*, in which the proud are 'scattered . . . in the imagination of their hearts' (Luke 1.51 AV). Such talk might appear to indicate avoidance as the more godly course, but that is one option that is emphatically not open to the religious believer, for we live by faith and not sight and so must be constantly directing our minds beyond the immediately visible or tangible into hints of other worlds and other realities. The point in those negative scriptural judgments was surely not that the imagination is inherently evil, but rather that without some guidance, like all God's gifts, it can be misused, even badly so. Indeed, in most modern translations some other word is usually substituted! However, if the imagination is directed by what God has revealed of the divine nature through biblical revelation and the created world, then the necessary aids are already in place to ensure, potentially at least, a rich exploration of how this material world might point beyond itself to that greater reality that is God.

Such use of images is of course fundamental to Scripture itself, as Ed Henderson so lucidly illustrates in his discussion of the work of Austin Farrer, but it would be a sad day for the Church were matters left there and no attempt made to bring those same (and related) images into living contact with modern culture. It is this task that is attempted so finely here, as the more directly artistic work of other friends of C. S. Lewis is explored. What emerges most clearly is the way in which imagination is anything but a flight from the harsh realities of this world. Thus Ann Loades stresses the effect of two world wars on the imagery of Dorothy L. Sayers, David Hein the impact of an illicit love affair on Rose Macaulay's *Towers of Trebizond*, Ralph C. Wood the integration of sorrow and joy in the fiction of J. R. R. Tolkien, and Charles Hefling how the greatest truths for Charles Williams come through the descent into Hell. Even Lewis himself, as Peter J. Schakel observes, had to wrestle with his instinctive distrust of the imagination before reaching a more nuanced position in which it has become an indispensable adjunct to reason.

Charles Hefling takes as his motto a famous quotation from W. H. Auden, that it is thanks to the Incarnation that 'the imagination is redeemed from promiscuous fornication with its own images'. Precisely because faith provides some direction for the Christian's imagination, fiction written under that inspiration will still engage with truth. Although carrying us well beyond the world we know, it will yet remain firmly anchored in a world where sorrow and despair are firmly faced even as they are, as they were in Christ's own life, transfigured into hope and joy. It is the way in which both the original authors and their present commentators encourage us toward just such a vision that makes these essays so important and so stimulating for further reflection.

David Brown
University of St Andrews

Introduction:
Faith, reason and imagination

DAVID HEIN AND EDWARD HENDERSON

To many people, faith means giving cognitive assent to religious claims that seem impossible to credit in our scientific age. A widely used dictionary offers the following as its first definition of 'faith': 'unquestioning belief that does not require proof or evidence'.[1] Indeed, to some Christians, faith means straining every nerve to believe doctrinal propositions – creedal assertions such as 'born of the Virgin Mary' – in the face of rational evidence to the contrary. God, they hope, will eventually reward their pious efforts – their credulity, their 'faith' – by granting them everlasting life in heaven. And that, they are confident, is basically what the Christian religion is all about.

Like many views of Christianity in the popular mind, this understanding of faith is unhistorical and misleading, not to mention theologically and morally questionable. Better always to recall what the Lutheran theologian Joseph Sittler used to say: Christians were celebrating before they were cerebrating. Images (such as the pregnant image of the Supper, which Austin Farrer explores so richly), stories (of the Crucifixion, for example) and worship (proclaiming Jesus as Lord) came first. Doctrine (such as the Chalcedonian definition of the Person of Christ) grew out of the experiences and reflections of early Christians in their communities.

Before they set forth a doctrine of the Trinity, Christians were experiencing Christ as saviour, worshipping the Son as divine, and predicating of him powers and prerogatives appropriate only to God; they were experiencing the Spirit in their midst, guiding, inspiring, teaching, convincing. Faith as trust in this person, Jesus, was foundational; faith as intellectual assent to creedal propositions came later. Doctrine, the Scottish theologian David Brown has rightly said, is 'secondary and parasitic on the stories and images that give religious belief its shape and vitality'.[2]

1

Better, in fact, to think of the life of faith rather than of faith on its own, for 'living a life' brings to mind the responsive, active side of faith. Thus: faith not as affirming difficult doctrines but as living into Christian truth-claims and discovering their meaning by doing the will of God. Faith as loyalty to the One God beyond the many gods and to this One God's cause. Faith as a trusting hope in God's future. Faith as the opposite not of doubt but of fear: faith courageously taking doubt within itself. Faith as the habitual orientation of a self whose character has been formed by images and stories and shaped by practices that sink these images deep within a person's mind and heart and will. Faith, then, as a dynamic involvement of the whole self and not an affair of any one aspect of the self – cognitive, volitional or emotional – alone.

Nor should faith be claimed as an accomplishment of the self in isolation from other selves, working out its separate peace with God. Faith means living a grateful life embedded in a community of forgiven sinners still *in via*. Indeed, faith points to self-forgetfulness rather than to self-assertion and individual achievement. Faith means loving God and neighbour in response to God's love for us. Christianity, therefore, should be seen as a religion to be practised, a faith to be lived, and not as a rigid system of doctrine. It is, in other words, a form of life that requires – in order to be truly grasped – the engagement of the imagination, the senses and the intellect.[3]

Faith and reason – *pace* some secularists – are not enemies; nor are they ships passing in the night. The faculty of reason enables us to think and to form judgments. More precisely, reason refers to our ability to analyse, to think systematically, to form concepts and to argue in a logical way. The rational faculty is concerned with the products of empirical discovery (perception) or with the results of logical analysis. While the imagination deals in concrete particulars, reason moves toward abstractions. Imagination integrates; reason analyses. Imagination thrives on creativity; reason is content to observe and deduce.[4]

Imagination may be a concept less familiar and hence harder to grasp than either faith or reason. In a sense, we know imagination when we see it; or, rather, we know it when we experience its effects. Consider two sermons. They have the same factual matter; they make the same logical argument. Outlines of their underlying doctrinal content would overlap completely; a bare-bones précis of one would look just like a précis of the other. But the first sermon strikes us as dry and underwhelming; the preacher leaves ideas hanging out in mid-air somewhere between pulpit and pew. The second strikes home in a way that makes connections to our lives; it even turns out to be – memorable. David Brown observes that although facts 'sometimes attract our attention', it is the imagination that brings out their significance for us: 'It is through appealing to our imagination that they are enabled to become "truths for us", as it were.'[5] The first preacher competently laid out the facts, but the second one revealed their meaning for us in our everyday lives; and her extra effort made all the difference. A large part of the achievement of the imaginative writers discussed in this book is their success not simply in stating facts but in showing us how the truths of faith can live in the particularities of our own lives.

The friends of C. S. Lewis recognized him as a master of the art of using vivid imagery to connect old truths with contemporary life. He spoke of the Incarnation, for example, not in a way that supplanted Scripture but in a manner that heightened his listeners' sense of this event's relevance for their own time.[6] Thus, in his *Broadcast Talks*, Lewis described God as 'landing in this enemy-occupied world in disguise and starting a sort of secret society to undermine the devil'.[7] Lewis never wished or claimed to say anything new about the Christian faith. What was fresh and invigorating was the way he brought together imagination and facts. His wartime analogy could not have failed to alert those who, worriedly residing in the UK in the early 1940s, confronted a very real enemy whose plans of conquest and domination were quickly being realized.[8]

Although we speak of imagination as an individual faculty, the theologian David Harned reminds us that imagination may be thought of not as 'a single power . . . of the self, still less merely the source of its dreams and fantasies', but as 'the sum of all the resources within us that we employ to form accurate images of the self and its world'. As a specialist in Christian ethics, Harned finds images and imagination useful precisely in their distinctive ability to enable human beings to see themselves and others – both their strengths and their weaknesses – more clearly: thereby to equip and empower persons for richer life in the real world. Even when imagination's genre is creative fiction, its task is still to discover 'potentiality and new possibilities' for the self, because 'it is oriented first . . . toward actuality.

3

Where else indeed could genuine possibilities be found?' At their best, he says, images represent the self and its world, actual or possible, in a fashion 'that has an immediacy and concreteness which conceptualizations lack'. Because they are concrete, 'images are more important for the exercise of human agency than are conceptual prescriptions'.[9]

David Harned reminds us that images and imagination enable us to make moral decisions because 'we are free to act in some purposive fashion only within the world that we can see. Before our decisions, supporting our approach to moral life, distinguishing us from our neighbors, there is our way of seeing . . .' Our perceptions shape our decisions, for good or ill; and how we see is 'a function of our character, of the history and habits of the self, and ultimately of the stories that we have heard and with which we identify ourselves'. The ways in which we see, Harned notes, are 'determined by the constellation of images . . . that resides within the household of the self'.[10]

A person might naturally infer, however, that because the imagination has to do with forming 'images', it is therefore concerned with mere appearances rather than with underlying reality.[11] But that is not what distinguishes imagination from reason. David Brown notes that 'there need not be any necessary conflict between the resources of reason and of the imagination', for both can provide 'access to the truth'.[12] What imagination offers is something alluded to in our earlier description of effective and ineffective preaching and vividly demonstrated in examples from C. S. Lewis and his friends: the power to make connections. The imagination, Brown points out, 'has one undoubted advantage over either reason or ordinary perception in its ability . . . to think laterally, to allow combinations that are not themselves necessarily present either in the mind or in nature'. Sometimes imagination will follow a trail that leads nowhere, but often 'image and metaphor can help detect connections that had not previously been identified'.[13]

According to Peter J. Schakel, who has written at length on reason and imagination in C. S. Lewis's work, imagination meant various things to Lewis. Most of all, Lewis understood this faculty to be concerned with the discernment of meaning. Reason finds factual truth, but imagination and metaphor are necessary in order to fully grasp the significance of truth.[14] For Lewis, reason is, in Schakel's words, 'the capacity for analysis, abstraction, logical deductions'; while imagination is 'the image-making, fictionalizing, integrative power'.[15] Both must be present 'in a balanced personality', Lewis believed: the 'clarity and strength of reason' complementing the 'beauty and creativity of imagination'.[16] Lewis saw that myth has the capacity to achieve and present this balanced perspective: by 'joining the outside view with the inside view, contemplation with enjoyment, and the rational with the imaginative'.[17] In sum, 'Imagination, for Lewis, can be defined as the mental, but not intellectual, faculty that puts things into meaningful relationships to form unified wholes.' Imagination accomplishes this feat 'not through a logical or intellectual process but through association, intuition, or inspiration'. Examples are easy to spot when we look around us. Composers of music connect notes and themes in ways that are both fresh and unified; visual artists arrange lines and colours to form new, integrated compositions; writers bring together not only words but also images and sounds to express emotions, characters, thoughts and experiences in arresting ways.[18] Thereby, Schakel says, 'Imaginative experience enables us to enter the lives of others while yet remaining ourselves.'[19]

C. S. Lewis knew, however, that most of us are not creative artists. Instead, we are listeners, observers and readers – in fact, ordinary mortals trying to make sense of our lives and of the world around us. Fortunately, Lewis was primarily concerned not with imaginative producers but with imaginative receivers. Thus he thought deeply and wrote carefully about ways to nourish imagination so that more people would be equipped to grasp essential truths for living.[20]

In Christianity, the ordinary believer is assisted on this path to greater awareness and enlargement of being through what we can call the 'sacramental imagination'. This centrally important way of construing reality is based on the idea that in the Incarnation, in the words of a Roman Catholic theologian, 'God in Christ addresses us as a human being among human beings, thus making all of human life and every human encounter potentially revelatory of the grace of God.'[21] Christian faith is not the belief that certain abstract ideas are true; it is a lived relationship with a God who has come and still comes in the particularities of life. To recognize and engage with the effective presence of God in the midst of these particulars, imagination is not just helpful; it is necessary: 'the immediacy of God's presence to our souls', said the theologian John Baillie, 'is a mediated immediacy'.[22] As mediators of divine presence, images are sacramental.

According to one Lewis scholar, because Lewis was a 'sacrament-alist', he believed that 'Reality tends toward the concrete.' Attempts to apprehend reality, this scholar notes in summarizing Lewis's view, 'are very far from being exhausted by [the] logical, the discursive, or the propositional' – that is, by reason alone. Hence, 'Lewis, for all of his rigorous and remorselessly logical manner of pursuing an argument, was at bottom a "catholic".' The sacramental imagination is closely related to faith's ability to apprehend reality, for 'that which faith grasps is characteristically mediated to us via solid images, most notably the Incarnation.'[23]

Imagination, therefore, is necessary because reality is a reality of particulars, not of generalities. No one has ever seen humankind in general, only particular persons. Love your neighbour as yourself; live by faith in hope with love; do not bury your talent in a field out of fear; do not use religious practices as a way to show off and gain the approval of people; and so on. These scriptural teachings must be lived in a world vastly different in its concrete particulars from the world in which Jesus and the earliest Church lived. As abstract principles they do not carry instructions within themselves about how to live them in the concreteness of our world now. Further abstractions cannot help; imagination must intervene. Therefore, Lewis and friends use their imaginative genius to show how the faith of the scriptural world is not limited to the world in which it arose but can be lived in other worlds, including especially our own.

In Christianity, as David Brown has clearly demonstrated, imagination, not historical fact alone, is crucial to the development and discernment of revealed truth. But he issues a realistic, historically grounded word of caution: imagination is not an infallible guide to right doctrine. Indeed, its effect can sometimes be stultifying, and he provides examples from past centuries of the misprisions of imagination. The human understanding of revealed truth can be enriched by imagination, but the products of this imagination must also be tested against doctrine.[24]

For all their keen appreciation of the wonders of a vital imagination, C. S. Lewis and his friends realized that imagination is not enough; in fact it can become dangerously subjective. Self-centred, it may spend all its time spinning illusions and aiding escape, taking the seeker not closer to truth but farther from it. In such cases, the imagination does not connect with the actual but instead misleads, disabling the self in its efforts to grasp reality. Excessively indulged, this imagination – a factory of wish-fulfilling fantasy – takes a person in the wrong direction, toward moral failure and spiritual decay. Examples of deluded characters, engaged in self-absorbed reveries and convinced of their own wisdom or heroism or martyrdom or deep spirituality, abound not only in Lewis's fiction but also in that of Tolkien, Williams and Macaulay. Sometimes persons do become 'scattered . . . in the imagination of their hearts'.[25] Therefore, imagination needs to be balanced by – and to work with – reason and facts, as faith seeks understanding.[26]

Clive Staples Lewis (1898–1963) eventually came to see the import-ance of a balance between reason and imagination. In the first chapter, Peter J. Schakel examines the development of Lewis's ideas about these powerful human faculties, tracing how the two sides of his person – the imaginative and the reasoning – grew and changed, but remained in tension with each other. In his twenties, Lewis, influenced by an old-fashioned, nineteenth-century rationalism, believed in a Coleridgean sense of Imagination (with a capital 'I') as Spiritual Awareness, and he held an elevated sense of Reason. Both strands of his person contributed to his conversion to theism, then to Christianity, in 1929–31; and his conversion changed his ideas about both.

Dropping the capital letters, Lewis adopted a lower view of reason and imagination as complementary and equally necessary pursuits, reason being the organ of truth, imagination the organ of meaning. Reason and imagination in complementary fashion appear in his writings about Christianity and in his fiction, but not initially in equal balance: in the 1940s he privileges reason, showing a greater trust and confidence in it; but in the 1950s the balance shifts as he places more confidence in imagination, and especially in myth as a powerful and meaningful literary form. His last imaginative works, *Till We Have Faces* and *Letters to Malcolm*, are arguably his best. In them he shows the limits of reason and both the use and the misuse of imagination in the acquisition and living of faith.

Austin Farrer (1904–68) differs from the other friends in that his thought about the power of imagination was focused largely on Scripture. Edward Henderson considers Farrer in explicit relation to Lewis's thought about the power of myth as it was expressed in Lewis's

1944 essay 'Myth Became Fact'. By explaining Farrer's answers to several philosophical questions, Henderson shows how Farrer saw the master images of Scripture not as accidental ways of presenting truths that could be known apart from the images but as the very form of understanding by which persons have engaged with God and through which God makes God's Self known. Henderson goes on to argue that the Christian Myth or Story can be reasonably believed to be true because the imagery in which its understanding of reality is carried satisfies what Farrer believed was the supreme aim of reason: to know 'what is most worthy of love and most binding on conduct', and to know it not as an intellectual exercise but in a way of life in which God is engaged and believers made more truly lovers of God and neighbour.[27] The images of Scripture, however, come from other times and places than our own. The continued vitality of the Christian faith requires that the Christian story enable faithful engagement with God in our own world. Bringing the old old story into the present world is precisely the work of imagination, and it is the work to which Lewis and his fiction-writing friends dedicated themselves.

To our present world, in which it is common to regard doctrinal commitments as unimportant and attachment to them even as perverse, Dorothy L. Sayers and Charles Williams are very clear: such Christian doctrines as creation *ex nihilo*, the Incarnation, Trinity and Atonement are not abstractions to be thought so much as patterns of life to be lived.

Dorothy L. Sayers (1893–1957) directly faced the hardships, destruction and moral challenges of the two world wars. Indeed, she did much of her theological thinking while reading Dante in the bomb shelters. Ann Loades traces the development of Sayers's work, showing us how in detective fiction, addresses, essays and plays, Sayers made herself and her readers face the pervasive effects of war and the fact of universal guilt. In the late 1930s Sayers began to write plays in order to put central Christian dogma literally on the stage. Loades shows us how Sayers, in her 1946 play *The Just Vengeance*, presents the idea of substitutionary atonement as anything but an angry God's bloody vengeance. There Sayers takes us to 'the place of the images' in and through which God makes God's Self present and lets us see the substitution as a divine action full of grace, beauty and joy.[28]

Charles Williams (1886–1945) shared with Sayers the conviction that Christian doctrine is essentially important, presenting it as descriptive of the facts in the drama of the soul's choice. In his chapter on Williams, theologian Charles Hefling discusses a writer whose work deals with 'the most significant experiences anyone can have' – to love and forgive, to be loved and forgiven. Concerned with helping people to see something of what it means to have a Christian apprehension of the wholeness of things, Williams, like Sayers, sees dogma as vital and illuminating, not boring: theological doctrine uncovers the great facts of existence. Through his writings, Williams aims to give his readers a sense of what he calls 'the pattern of the glory' of God. In its own way, his fiction can be compared to Dante's *Divine Comedy*, which he greatly admired.

Thus, for example, in his comprehensive theology, Williams shows how romantic love can take *caritas* within itself. Indeed, the events in the soul of the romantic lover become isomorphic with the events of the Gospel narrative and the Incarnation. Co-inherence – characteristic of the Incarnation, of the Trinity and of the Church – can also characterize in fact, as it already does in principle, the relations of human beings as members one of another. Something like the substitution that lies at the heart of the Atonement may be witnessed in striving to bear one another's burdens, reflected most deeply in the event of forgiveness: a remembering (not a simple forgetting) that moves ahead and does not hold grudges. Williams embraces the redeemed imagination, which discovers meaning not in solitary striving but as it finds its place within the co-inherent 'pattern of the glory'. Its images are worded meanings, embodied accuracies, which are ordered in relation to the meaning-filled and meaning-conferring reality of the Incarnation. This event grounds ordinary human existence – enabling it to find its place – because incarnation means the presence of God in the human which is at the same time the taking of humanity into God.

Rose Macaulay (1881–1958) stands in a more ambiguous relation to Christian doctrine than do Sayers and Williams. David Hein focuses his chapter on her last, highly acclaimed novel, *The Towers of Trebizond* (1956) and on her personal biography. Interpreting the novel through her biography, Hein presents us with a story that speaks with special poignancy to those modern seekers who are both inside and outside the Christian religion and who are especially in need of seeing how faith can be lived in the modern world.[29] Here they will find insights into obstacles to belief and into the relation of faith and doubt. They will also see the connection between these themes and Macaulay's appreciation of the ethos of the Church of England, including Anglicanism's high view of both reason and imagination.

Making these connections requires the engagement of the faculty of imagination, which, Macaulay believed, can take persons deeper into, not farther from, the actualities of existence. In the life of this writer, readers will notice the development of an imagination that becomes frankly and energetically sacramental, as Macaulay in her final years came more and more to treasure the riches of the Christian heritage and to participate in Christianity's embrace of matter and spirit together. But readers hoping to relax into a simple enjoyment of this major minor novelist would be advised to stay alert, for there may be surprises in store: Macaulay was a writer on the edge of this group of Christian friends. She declined pat answers, and, even after her reconversion, her quest remained restless.

Anchoring these explorations of faith and the power of imagination is Ralph C. Wood's reading of J. R. R. Tolkien (1892–1973). Wood considers Tolkien's grand *Legendarium*, which extends beyond *The Lord of the Rings* to include *The Silmarillion* and related stories, taking them as Tolkien himself conceived them, as parts of one comprehensive work. Here, then, in Tolkien is perhaps imagination's most sweeping Christian vision of the modern era. Wood shows how reality as Tolkien imagines it is reality as Christians must understand it now. It is especially appropriate for our time because it incorporates truth learned by Tolkien from the ancient Northern legends and myths, where life is shadowed by a melancholy sense of fate and by inexorable death, defeat and sorrow.

The truth Tolkien learned from the Northern myths is truth we may also learn from Darwin, Heisenberg and others who have made it impossible to deny the prevalence of accident, chaos and unpredictability in a world that includes an abundance of pain and suffering which cannot be glibly assigned to a clear divine plan. Yet in *The Lord of the Rings* Tolkien infuses the inescapable sorrow of this world with a still profounder sense of hope and joy, which can be experienced even now in lives that walk faithfully and supportively together. Faithful persons renounce the will to coercive power over others and live instead by the sacrificial embrace of hope, mutual fidelity, courage and non-coercive love, facing many sorrows within the bounds of time but happy to play parts in the great Drama in which good will not be finally defeated.

Notes

1 *Webster's New World College Dictionary*, 3rd edn, ed. Victoria Neufeldt (New York: Macmillan, 1996), p. 487.
2 David Brown, *Tradition and Imagination: Revelation and Change* (Oxford: Oxford University Press, 2004), p. 2.
3 David Brown, *God and Mystery in Words: Experience through Metaphor and Drama* (Oxford: Oxford University Press, 2008), pp. 277, 278.
4 Peter J. Schakel, *Reason and Imagination in C. S. Lewis: A Study of 'Till We Have Faces'* (Grand Rapids, MI: Eerdmans, 1984), p. 183 n. 2.
5 Brown, *Tradition and Imagination*, p. 283.
6 Brown, *God and Mystery in Words*, p. 116.
7 C. S. Lewis, *Broadcast Talks* (London: Geoffrey Bles, 1942), p. 61.
8 David Hein, 'A Note on C. S. Lewis's *The Screwtape Letters*', *The Anglican Digest* 49, no. 2 (2007), pp. 55–8.
9 David Baily Harned, *Images for Self-Recognition: The Christian as Player, Sufferer and Vandal* (New York: Seabury, 1977), p. 2.
10 David Baily Harned, *Faith and Virtue* (Philadelphia: United Church Press, 1973), pp. 29–30.
11 David Brown, *Discipleship and Imagination: Christian Tradition and Truth* (Oxford: Oxford University Press, 2004), p. 347.
12 Brown, *Discipleship and Imagination*, p. 352.
13 Brown, *Discipleship and Imagination*, p. 352.
14 Schakel, *Reason and Imagination*, p. 197 n. 26.
15 Schakel, *Reason and Imagination*, p. x.
16 Schakel, *Reason and Imagination*, p. 180.
17 Schakel, *Reason and Imagination*, p. 139.
18 Peter J. Schakel, *Imagination and the Arts in C. S. Lewis: Journeying to Narnia and Other Worlds* (Columbia: University of Missouri Press, 2002), pp. 4–5.
19 Schakel, *Imagination and the Arts*, p. 15.
20 Schakel, *Imagination and the Arts*, p. 11.
21 Mark R. Francis, 'Sacramental Theology', in *The Blackwell Encyclopedia of Modern Christian Thought*, ed. Alister E. McGrath (Oxford: Blackwell, 1995), p. 585.
22 John Baillie, *Our Knowledge of God* (London: Oxford University Press, 1939), p. 181.

23 Corbin Scott Carnell, 'Imagination', in *The C. S. Lewis Readers' Encyclopedia*, ed. Jeffrey D. Schultz and John G. West (Grand Rapids, MI: Zondervan, 1998), p. 214.

24 Brown, *Discipleship and Imagination*, pp. 261–70.

25 Luke 1.51 AV.

26 Schakel, *Imagination and the Arts*, pp. 21, 172–3.

27 Austin Farrer, *The End of Man*, ed. Charles C. Conti (London: SPCK, 1973), p. 157.

28 Dorothy L. Sayers, *The Just Vengeance* (London: Victor Gollancz, 1946), p. 47.

29 Brown, *Tradition and Imagination*, p. 367.

Figure 1 C. S. Lewis.
Photo by Arthur Strong © Ingrid Franzon.

1

C. S. Lewis: Reason, imagination and knowledge

PETER J. SCHAKEL

In May 1962, Margaret E. Rose of the School Broadcasting Department, British Broadcasting Corporation, wrote to C. S. Lewis: 'We are doing a series for Sixth Forms in the Autumn of 1962 called "Knowledge, Imagination and Truth" in which we hope to demonstrate the separate functions and the interplay of "reason" and "imagination" as means of knowledge. I . . . wonder whether you would be interested in doing the two talks on J. R. R. Tolkien's "The Lord of the Rings".'[1] Lewis replied: 'Many thanks . . . but I am afraid I must refuse. I am making a slow recovery from a serious illness, and have been warned by my doctor that in future I must refrain from all avoidable exertion.'[2] Readers of Lewis must wish that he had been able to complete this task and indeed must wonder what he would have written. Speculation on what Lewis's two talks would have said lies outside the scope of this essay, but I will attempt to indicate the lines of thought along which he would have worked.

What he would have said in 1962 about reason and imagination was not what he would have said in the 1920s. His basic presuppositions changed, and so did his understanding of reason and imagination and of the interplay between them. To understand the lines of thought along which he would have worked in the talks for Margaret Rose, we must begin by tracing those developments – beginning with imagination – which he said were important for him since his childhood.

When Lewis was six, seven and eight, he 'was living almost entirely in [his] imagination', he writes in his autobiography, *Surprised by Joy*: 'imagination of one sort or another played the dominant part' in those early years.[3] He goes on in that chapter to distinguish four different uses of the term 'imagination'. He does not mention one that is usually given as the initial definition: 'forming mental images

15

of things not actually present'.[4] The first one he does mention is imagination as reverie, daydream or fantasies of wish-fulfilment, that is, forming mental images of oneself as one wishes to be, at least for that moment. Lewis says he often indulged in wish-fulfilment fantasies, picturing himself cutting a fine figure (p. 15). This imaginative notion of himself presumably led him later to aspire to 'knuttery', wearing flashy clothes and plastering his hair with oil (p. 67).

Second is imagination as 'invention', or what classical rhetorical theory called 'discovery', the finding out or selection of topics to be treated or arguments to be used. This use of the term is closer than fantasizing to what Lewis thought of as imagination and is more important. Invention involves the making up – or discovery (such making up is not always conscious and deliberate) – of characters and plot in telling a story or of metaphors used in poetry or prose (p. 15).[5] Lewis began employing invention in childhood, as he wrote the Animal-Land stories which he describes at considerable length in *Surprised by Joy*, chiefly in chapters 1 and 5. It became very significant to him later as he wrote narrative poetry and prose fiction.

Lewis's interest focuses not on these three common uses of the term but on two less common (he might say higher) uses. First is 'poetic imagination', which he calls in 1955 'the highest sense of all' (p. 16), having an importance he says he already recognized in childhood. Lewis distinguishes between invention and poetic imagination when he says that his Animal-Land stories were training him to be 'a novelist; not a poet' (p. 15). The organic and intuitive power needed to write poetry (and myth) rises to a higher level than invention. It relies on 'inspiration' or 'genius'. It is the mental, but not intellectual, faculty that puts things into surprising and meaningful relationships to form unified wholes. The best poetry operates at a level beyond images. Ideally it is beyond words and in this sense is akin to music, the highest art form, which, without words, can be 'a sort of madness' in the strength of its effects.[6] Poetry uses metaphor or myth to lift a work (whether in prose or verse) beyond events or ideas, to make it 'profound and suggestive', to enable it to evoke extraordinary affective power and impact.[7] When Lewis says that he was living 'almost entirely in [his] imagination' (p. 15), he means that he was spending much of his time reading works of poetic and mythic imagination and being caught up in the powerful impressions created by them.

The final kind of imagination described in *Surprised by Joy* is Romantic imagination, the experience which in *The Pilgrim's Regress* Lewis calls Romanticism and in his autobiography he calls Joy. It is an experience of an acute, even painful, but desired, longing for the renewal of an experience of transcendent bliss. It occurs as the memory of an earlier moment involving bliss or beauty is triggered by a current experience of bliss or beauty. Lewis's first such experience occurred early in his life, as the sight of a flowering currant bush on a summer day joined with the memory of the first beauty Lewis ever knew, a toy garden his brother created in the lid of a biscuit tin. Such experiences, evoked by scenes of nature, music and poetry, became a foundational aspect of his life. He longed deeply, but could not determine what he was longing for, often mistaking intermediate objects for the ultimate object. 'By the imaginative life', he says when he describes the renewal of this experience in his teens after a long absence, 'I here mean only my life as concerned with Joy'; later he refers to 'the imaginative longing for Joy, or rather the longing which *was* Joy' (pp. 78–9, 175).

Joy is ultimately a longing for unity, though unity with what may be unclear. It is imaginative in that it is often set in motion by literature or music, which are products of the imagination. It involves being transported beyond the physical and emotional to a rapturous state that could take place only in the imagination at an inspired level. And it usually depends on memory, as the image of a remembered experience triggers a longing not for the past but for something of which a past experience is a symbol. Imagination in this sense is of crucial importance in Lewis's life as one of the reasons for his return to Christianity, as he came to the realization that the ultimate object of his longings was God, to be in the presence of God; but that understanding did not come until his early thirties. *Surprised by Joy* is in large part a celebration of the Romantic imagination, in its deepest and broadest sense.

At the same time that he was living in the imagination, he was developing his ability to reason. Presumably his ability to think logically went back to his home life. His father was a lawyer, 'fond of oratory', with 'great quickness of mind', and his mother was a 'promising mathematician' (p. 4). Lewis must have heard logical reasoning illustrated regularly as he listened to adult conversations in his home. Beyond that, his first schoolmaster, Robert Capron, bad as he was personally and pedagogically, taught geometry well and 'forced us to reason . . . I have been the better for those geometry lessons all my life' (p. 29). Critical thinking was a factor in his decision to reject the Christian faith in his early teens: he could not continue to accept what he was being taught: that a thousand non-Christian religions were sheer illusion, all except 'our own, the thousand and first, [which was] labelled True' (p. 63).

Lewis's ability and inclination to think analytically were greatly strengthened by the two years he spent being tutored by W. T. Kirkpatrick, 'a "Rationalist" of the old, high and dry nineteenth-century type', a man who came close to being a purely logical entity (pp. 139, 135). By encountering and engaging with Kirkpatrick's ruthless dialectic, Lewis's reason was honed and became razor sharp. As Lewis says, 'I loved ratiocination . . . [and] became a not contemptible sparring partner' (p. 137). Reason and logic exerted a strong influence on all aspects of Lewis's life from then on.

Lewis describes his mind in his late teens as torn between imagination and reason: 'The two hemispheres of my mind were in the sharpest contrast. On the one side a many-islanded sea of poetry and myth; on the other a glib and shallow "rationalism". Nearly all I loved I believed to be imaginary; nearly all that I believed to be real I thought grim and meaningless' (p. 170). He was torn partly because he could not, at this point, resolve their conflicting claims to truth and knowledge. When he returned to Oxford after service in the First World War, he still felt divided, devoting his academic pursuits to reading philosophy (reason), while using his spare time to write poetry (imagination).

This dividedness is the subject of one of Lewis's most intriguing poems, 'Reason': 16 lines, undated and not published during his life. In it Lewis contrasts the cool clarity and strength of reason (symbolized by Athene, the 'maid' of the poem) with the warm darkness and creativity of the imagination (Demeter, the earth-mother, in the poem). The poem concludes:

> Oh who will reconcile in me both maid and mother,
> Who make in me a concord of the depth and height?
> Who make imagination's dim exploring touch
> Ever report the same as intellectual sight?
> Then could I truly say, and not deceive,
> Then wholly say, that I BELIEVE.[8]

Reason is clear and pure and stable; there is nothing indulgent or lax or compromising about her. The imagery used for it in the poem is celestial, which implies that it can be sinned against, not just in the sense that one human being can wrong another but also in the sense of a violation of divine expectations. By contrast, the imagery given to imagination is dark and seductive: she is desirable, even sexually appealing, and thus has a slightly dangerous and questionable character. The imagery suggests a strong opposition between reason and imagination. Lewis sees positive elements in both – the clarity and strength of reason, the beauty and creativity of imagination – and he recognizes that both must be present in a balanced personality. Thus he urges the reader to 'Tempt not Athene' and to 'Wound not in her fertile pains / Demeter, nor rebel against her mother-right'. The poet longs for something that will ease the tension in their relationship, but such a total harmony of intellect and imagination would be difficult when the two elements are as strongly opposed as they appear to be here. It seems likely that the poem was written in the late 1920s and reflects his personal situation then, as he struggled with the role that reason and imagination should have in his academic and religious life.

The opposite pulls of imagination and reason must have been particularly intense for Lewis in his twenties. When he returned from the war at age 19, his ambition was to become a great poet, thus to live in the realm of poetic imagination. As his close friend Owen Barfield put it, 'At that time, if you thought of Lewis, you automatically thought of poetry.'[9] Lewis published a slender volume of poems, *Spirits in Bondage*, in 1919 and a long narrative poem, *Dymer*, in 1926, both under the pseudonym Clive Hamilton, and he wrote a great deal of verse while completing his rigorously intellectual academic work. His desire to live in poetic imagination evolved into an intellectual interest in the nature and effects of imagination, partly because this was a contentious subject at the time. Lewis's friend Barfield and his soon-to-be antagonist I. A. Richards each published in the mid-1920s a book which had imagination at its centre.[10]

This deepening interest led Lewis to engage in an extended, highly philosophical dispute with Barfield in the 1920s about the nature and theory of imagination. Lewis dubbed the dispute 'The Great War' – a war because they fought over whether imagination was a way of attaining truth, as Barfield believed, or was not, as Lewis held. The war was carried on in letters, in several treatises, and in face-to-face discussions, exploring the definition of imagination and its conceptual foundations.[11] In a series of fine articles, Stephen Thorson has analysed the Great War documents and reached important conclusions regarding Lewis's ideas about reason and the imagination in them.[12]

The starting point for understanding changes that took place in Lewis's ideas because of the Great War is that imagination cannot be considered in isolation. As Barfield put it, a theory of imagination 'must concern itself, whether positively or negatively, with its relation to truth'.[13] Lewis's ideas about imagination, Thorson believes, must be examined in the context of his metaphysics (what we are) and his epistemology (how we know). In his Great War, pre-conversion years, Lewis believed that a human being is an evolving Spirit, and he held a high, Coleridgean (and Barfieldian) view of Imagination (with a capital 'I') as Spiritual Awareness, 'a consciousness' – in Thorson's words – 'of the soul's oneness with universal Spirit as well as the soul's oneness with the world of Nature'.[14] Thus, through Imagination, we can participate in Spirit.[15]

In Barfield's epistemology, Imagination is a method of attaining knowledge of spiritual reality (Truth with a capital 'T'). Lewis, however, starting from a different epistemology, disagreed. From the time he read Samuel Alexander's *Space, Time and Deity* (1920) in his early twenties, Lewis accepted Alexander's distinction between Enjoyment and Contemplation (both terms used in a special, technical sense). When one sees an object, one 'enjoys' the act of seeing and 'contemplates' the object; if one begins thinking about seeing, one contemplates the seeing and enjoys the thought. One cannot simultaneously focus attention on an object and on the self that is focusing attention. This distinction, Lewis says in *Surprised by Joy*, he accepted as soon as he read it; he regarded it thereafter as 'an indispensable tool of thought': 'You cannot hope and also think about hoping at the same moment; for in hope we look to hope's object and we interrupt this by (so to speak) turning round to look at the hope itself. Of course the two activities can and do alternate with great rapidity; but they are distinct and incompatible' (p. 218).

Barfield noticed a contradiction here. Metaphysically, Lewis affirmed oneness of soul and Spirit; but epistemologically he denied that oneness by saying that a person cannot simultaneously be Spirit (the contemplating self) and soul (the enjoying self). Therefore Barfield suggested that Lewis reject enjoyment versus contemplation and accept that Imagination is a source of Truth. Instead, Lewis rejected his belief in emerging Spirit and with it his belief in Imagination. As a result of this change, he switched from viewing humans as developing Spirits to regarding them as created beings, and he scaled back his high view of Imagination, coming to regard it as a lower faculty, 'able', Thorson says, 'to reflect spiritual values, but not "spiritual" itself'.[16] In his new view, imagination (now with a lower-case 'i') is no longer the highest human quality, though he still regarded it as a good and potentially valuable one. Imaginative experiences are not spiritual in themselves, though they may be an avenue leading toward the spiritual. With a metaphysic now compatible with his epistemology, Lewis could consistently hold that imagination is not the source of truth; instead, he came to view it as the source of meaning. To this crucial point we will return shortly.

At the same time that he was reconsidering and arriving at a new understanding of imagination, something similar was happening to his understanding of reason. In the mid-1920s, Lewis taught philosophy full-time for a year at University College and part-time in his early years at Magdalen College: 'I was now teaching philosophy (I suspect very badly) as well as English. And my watered Hegelianism wouldn't serve for tutorial purposes' (*Surprised by Joy*, p. 222). With the intellectual honesty and moral seriousness that always characterized him, he believed he needed to take his subject, and with it the use of reason, more seriously: 'A tutor must make things clear' (p. 222). That impulse was reinforced by a conversation he had with Barfield and Lewis's friend and former student Bede Griffiths:

> I happened to refer to philosophy as 'a subject'. 'It wasn't a subject to Plato,' said Barfield, 'it was a way.' The quiet but fervent agreement of Griffiths, and the quick glance of understanding between these two, revealed to me my own frivolity. Enough had been thought, and said, and felt, and imagined. It was about time that something should be done. (p. 225)

What needed to be done was to take reason seriously, to acknowledge that it exists not for playing intellectual games but for the pursuit of truth. And that acknowledgment became a contributing factor in his return to (or conversion to) Christianity, a process that involved reason and imagination acting in a complementary fashion.

A key step occurred as he rationally decided that 'an attempt at complete virtue must be made' (p. 226). He mentions this step in passing in *Surprised by Joy* but describes it in more detail in the first series of broadcast talks that he gave on BBC radio in 1942. 'Right and Wrong as a Key to the Meaning of the Universe' lays out the route Lewis himself followed in the late 1920s, using reason to reach a conviction about the existence of natural law and of a personal lawgiver behind that law. In the final talk of this series, Lewis notes: 'We have not yet got as far as the God of any actual religion, still less the God of that particular religion called Christianity. We have only got as far as a Somebody or Something behind the Moral Law', and done so through the use of empirical evidence and logical thinking.[17] At this point in his journey he had accepted as truth 'that there is a real Moral Law, and a Power behind the law, and that [Lewis had] broken that law and put [himself] wrong with that Power'.[18]

This awareness was sufficient to make him a theist, but not a Christian. He believed that he needed salvation, but he did not know how such salvation works or what 'being saved' means. His problem was that he could not grasp the nature of the Atonement, a divine mystery on which the Church Fathers advanced different theories and on which Christian denominations still differ. In *Mere Christianity* Lewis acknowledges that 'no explanation will ever be quite adequate to the reality' of the Atonement.[19] His failure to grasp this doctrine, he tells Arthur Greeves in 1931, was what had been holding him back for the past year or so from taking the step from theism to Christianity: what held him back was

> not . . . so much a diffculty in believing as a difficulty in knowing what the doctrine *meant*: you can't believe a thing while you are ignorant [of] *what* the thing is. My puzzle was the whole doctrine of Redemption: in what sense the life and death of Christ 'saved' or 'opened salvation to' the world.[20]

Lewis discovered that in order to be able to understand and accept the doctrines of Christianity, his reason needed the assistance of his imagination. This discovery occurred through a long conversation with Tolkien and Hugo Dyson late at night on 19–20 September 1931. He wrote about this evening to Greeves a few weeks later:

Now what Dyson and Tolkien showed me was this: that if I met the idea of sacrifice in a Pagan story I didn't mind it at all: ... in Pagan stories I was prepared to feel the myth as profound and suggestive of meanings beyond my grasp even tho' I could not say in cold prose 'what it meant'.

Now the story of Christ is simply a true myth: a myth working on us in the same way as the others, but with this tremendous difference that *it really happened*: and one must be content to accept it in the same way, remembering that it is God's myth where the others are men's myths: i.e. the Pagan stories are God expressing Himself through the minds of poets, using such images as He found there, while Christianity is God expressing Himself through what we call 'real things'.[21]

The interplay of reason and imagination is important here. Tolkien and Dyson convinced Lewis logically that his imaginative experience with pagan myth was analogous (a 'logic' word) to what is going on in Christianity. This analogy opened Lewis to feeling the profundity of Christ's death and to accepting it as true and meaningful, without needing to 'grasp' it or to explain intellectually 'what it meant'.

In a letter to Griffiths in 1936, Lewis wrote that 'you and I came to [Christianity] chiefly by Reason (I don't mean, of course, that any one comes at all but by God's grace – I am talking about the route not the motive power) ...'[22] Taking reason seriously involved regarding it in a new, post-conversion way. 'Doubtless, by definition, God was Reason itself' (*Surprised by Joy*, p. 228); or, as he puts it in a 1941 essay, 'Reason is divine', though the use of reason by imperfect human beings in a fallen world is not.[23] The post-conversion Lewis accepts that reason is the route to truth: 'By *Reason* I [mean] "the faculty whereby we recognise or attain necessary truths" or "the faculty of grasping self-evident truths or logically deducing those which are not self-evident".'[24]

This understanding of reason led to a new understanding of its relationship to the imagination. In a 1939 essay Lewis wrote these important sentences: 'For me, reason is the natural organ of truth; but imagination is the organ of meaning. Imagination, producing new metaphors or revivifying old, is not the cause of truth, but its condition.'[25] Here he has found the reconciliation of maid and mother, the concord of depth and height, that he was seeking when he wrote the poem 'Reason'. This understanding of the complementary nature of reason and imagination enabled him to move from theism to acceptance (or re-acceptance) of Christianity, and to become an extremely effective defender of Christianity and communicator about the Christian faith.

A one-sentence summary of Lewis's ideas regarding the interplay of reason and imagination is that reason and imagination are equally necessary and complementary in nature, one as the natural organ of truth, the other as the organ of meaning. This statement takes us back to the definitions of imagination in *Surprised by Joy* and helps to clarify why Lewis was not much interested in the usual, common definitions of the term but was interested in poetic imagination (the faculty with which a poet creates meaning, or through which meaning is revealed to the poet) and Romantic imagination (the faculty with which we receive meaning and seek unity with ultimate Meaning). Reason and imagination are complementary, but they are separate; and the interplay of the two is a means of attaining knowledge.

Lewis says that a desire for knowledge is one of the distinctive traits of the human being: Unlike 'the other animals ... he simply wants to know things, wants to find out what reality is like, simply for the sake of knowing'.[26] All our knowledge, Lewis says elsewhere, depends in varying proportions on authority, reason and experience.[27] The proportions differ depending on the kind of knowledge, whether knowledge *of* something by acquaintance or personal experience (*connaître*), or knowledge *about* something, analytically or abstractly (*savoir*).[28]

Abstract knowledge is attained by observation, by reasoning about what is observed and by authority (reported observation, deductive reasoning); imagination plays very little part in acquiring it. Lewis writes in 'Myth Became Fact': 'Human intellect is incurably abstract ... Yet the only realities we experience are concrete – this pain, this pleasure, this dog, this man.'[29] The word 'tree' is abstract; the tree outside my window is concrete. As Charlie W. Starr points out in a fine article, Lewis believed that the separations of this world (abstract/concrete, reason/imagination) keep us from ever knowing something completely: 'We can think about it; we can experience it. We cannot do both simultaneously.' In heaven, as Lewis thought of it, experiencing a thing and thinking about it 'would be a single, simultaneous activity', but not in this world.[30]

Imagination, through the invention of new metaphors or the re-vitalization of old ones, is needed to bridge the divide, to reconcile the opposites, to enable us to experience abstractions that otherwise we can be aware of only intellectually, only through reason.[31] 'For all of us', Lewis writes in 'Bluspels and Flalansferes', 'there are things which we cannot fully understand at all, but of which we can get a faint inkling by means of metaphor.'[32] Truth in this world, as Starr sums it up, is 'an abstract statement of correspondence with reality obtained by reason which operates in the abstract . . . Meaning, however, is a pro-duct of imaginative connection through metaphor . . . Whether or not a meaning corresponds to reality (whether or not it is true) is some-thing that must be determined by reason.'[33] Abstract knowledge relies on the interplay of reason and imagination: the one to determine truth, the other to provide access to the meaningfulness of such truth.

Knowledge by acquaintance relies less on reason and more on experience, and sometimes it has a more direct relationship to im-agination. We can gain such acquaintance through direct experience, but even reading or hearing about the experiences of others can result in a kind of knowledge if received with an active imagination. This awareness is not knowledge as *savoir*, Lewis explains in *An Experiment in Criticism*, but as *connaître*: 'we become . . . other selves' through the use of imaginative identification, and this enables us 'to see what [others] see, to occupy, for a while, their seat in the great theatre.'[34] Through 'reading great literature', he continues, 'I become a thousand men and yet remain myself.'[35] *An Experiment in Criticism* deals speci-fically with the role of imagination in reading literature, but its final pages imply that sympathetic imagination is not something that occurs only in books; imagination is also at work in a non-literary way when we have empathy with others and attempt to identify with their thoughts and feelings.

Myth, Lewis believed, takes all this to a higher level. It is, he says in 'Myth Became Fact', the partial solution to the separations of abstract and concrete: 'In the enjoyment of a great myth we come nearest to experiencing as a concrete what can otherwise be under-stood only as an abstraction.'[36] He illustrates this point by suggesting that we consider Orpheus and Eurydice as an example of the principle that one cannot both think about and experience something at the same time; he then goes on to meet the objection that we had never before attached this meaning to the ancient myth:

Of course not. You are not looking for an abstract 'meaning' at all. If that was what you were doing the myth would be for you no true myth but a mere allegory. You were not knowing, but tasting; but what you were tasting turns out to be a universal principle. The moment we *state* this principle, we are admittedly back in the world of abstraction. It is only while receiving the myth as a story that you experience the principle concretely.[37]

Experiencing an abstraction, a principle, concretely at first seems an oxymoron. But Lewis's point is that there are different kinds of concreteness: in an everyday sense, 'concrete' is what we apprehend with the senses. But there is a whole other realm of concreteness that we cannot apprehend with the senses, starting with 'the supreme example of the concrete', God.[38] Lewis illustrates this supra-sensible reality in *The Great Divorce*, with grass that pricks the feet of the ghosts visiting heaven and drops of water that pierce them like bullets; it is a realm where truth is not abstract, experienced only with the intellect, but concrete: 'You can taste it like honey and be embraced by it as by a bridegroom.'[39]

Myth takes us as close to that heavenly unity of abstract and concrete, grasped simultaneously with the reason and the imagination, as is attainable in this world: 'You [are] not knowing, but tasting ... What flows into you from the myth is not truth but reality (truth is always *about* something, but reality is that *about which* truth is).'[40] As Starr puts it, 'Myth solves the problem of knowing by removing abstraction from the equation ... The myth is a real object of thought, a sub-created, concrete reality, intended not to represent reality outside itself ... but to be simply what it is, a pattern of the reality behind (not a pattern about that reality but an actual taste of the reality itself).'[41] As soon as we try to put into words the meaning we have tasted through myth, however, we move into abstract statements, the realm of reason. In our world, then, both kinds of knowledge, *connaître* and *savoir*, need the complementary actions of reason and imagination. Reason relies on the imagination as well as experience (sensory, non-sensory, imaginary) to supply it with conceptions; while imagination needs reason to manipulate those conceptions, to discover what can be put together and what cannot, to judge what is true and what is not.

Lewis did not attempt to articulate a coherent, consistent theory of reason and imagination. To the extent that he had a theory, something like what is summarized above, he had it worked out before he was 40, after he had given up the dream of becoming a great poet and before he began writing most of his fiction. But it wasn't a fully worked out scheme, or at least not fully balanced. For example, he says, 'Doubtless, by definition, God was Reason itself', and 'Reason is divine'. But he never says, 'Doubtless, by definition, God was also Imagination itself', or 'Imagination is also divine'. Why not? Is imagination not a vehicle of God's self-revelation? The omission suggests a privileging of reason, a greater degree of trust in reason than in imagination. Fortunately, his practice came to exceed his theory, as he became increasingly comfortable with a larger role for the imagination.

Lewis's three major apologetic works – *The Problem of Pain* (1940), the radio talks of 1942–4 (reprinted as *Mere Christianity* in 1952) and *Miracles* (1947) – reflect the earlier stage with its privileging of reason. These works display increasing skilfulness in the use of dialectic in defending the Christian faith, along with a growing ability to employ imagination in making his ideas clear and appealing. Lewis is adept in the use of vivid, memorable images and analogies in his expository prose, one of the most famous appearing in *The Problem of Pain*: 'Pain insists on being attended to. God whispers to us in our pleasures, speaks in our conscience, but shouts in our pains: it is His megaphone to rouse a deaf world.'[42] In a letter a few years earlier, Lewis had said that such analogies are not truly or purely imaginative. Commenting on Jesus' parables, Lewis says their mode is intellectual rather than imaginative: 'like a philosopher's *illustration* rather than a poet's *simile*.'[43] He extends the point to ordinary speech: 'the poet uses images as such, because they are images: the ordinary man . . . uses them *faute de mieux* [for want of any better alternative] to attain knowledge, i.e. his end is the same as the philosopher's.'[44] In these statements, Lewis seems to limit the range of imagination, separating it sharply from intellect in a purist fashion; if an attempt to find images or analogies involves deliberation or the use of reason, it should not be considered imaginative.

Here his own example counteracts his theoretical statements. Finding apt and effective images and analogies does involve imagination, at least at the level of invention. But coming up with surprising and illuminating comparisons often goes beyond invention, beyond what is deliberate and under our control; some degree of 'inspiration' is involved. As Lewis puts it in talking about the use of metaphors for the sake of instruction, 'in practice very few metaphors can be purely magistral; only that which to some degree enlightens ourselves is likely to enlighten others'.[45] The imagination may be used in the service of reason, but this use is imaginative nonetheless. And this use fulfils imagination's role as the organ of meaning: the images and analogies Lewis includes complement the development of reasoned explanation and argument by bringing out its meaningfulness, rendering it more understandable and applicable.

The combination of reasoned thought and imaginative style addresses the whole person. What Lewis says of Jesus' approach applies in lesser fashion to his own approach. He objected to labelling Jesus as either a poet or a philosopher: 'The overwhelming majority of His utterances are in fact addressed neither to thought nor to the imagination but to the "heart" – i.e. to the will and the affections . . .'.[46] The best of Lewis's Christian and moral writings likewise are addressed to the heart.

His adult fictional writing starts with a work in which reason predominates over imagination. *The Pilgrim's Regress: An Allegorical Apology for Christianity, Reason and Romanticism* (1933) is an allegory, which of all the imaginative literary forms has the greatest tendency to rely on the intellect for the completion of its meaning and effect; and the word *Apology* in the title signals that the emphasis falls on intellect, not imagination. The three books involving Elwin Ransom are more effective imaginatively, though the fiction continues to be grounded in reasoned truths. *Out of the Silent Planet* (1938) tells a good story and has memorable and meaningful images (including the eldils). But the book's themes are spelled out in conceptual, not imaginative, terms, and Lewis himself referred to the story as a vehicle for smuggling theology into people's minds.[47] The final chapter of *Perelandra*, especially the description of the Great Dance, is high myth, 'a real object of thought, a sub-created, concrete reality, intended not to represent reality outside itself . . . but to be simply what it is, a pattern of the reality behind', to use again Starr's words quoted above. At the centre of the book, however, is an extended philosophical-theological discussion relying on reason which is simultaneously, implicitly, a critique of reason, showing that a defence against sophistry – the misuse of reason – can accomplish only so much. *That Hideous Strength* also rises to the highest levels of imagination in the magnificent passage relating the Descent of the Gods. But the exposure of evil and instruction in the good that suffuse the book are achieved largely through mini-essays, developing in a few sentences reasoned arguments that in some cases Lewis had earlier expounded in full-length essays.

In later years Lewis seems to become increasingly comfortable with and confident in his use of imagination. His works dealing with the Christian faith are less argumentative and assertive than the earlier ones; they rely more on experience and imagination and permit the reader more freedom of response. The very titles of his later books on Christianity (*Reflections on the Psalms* and *Letters to Malcolm: Chiefly on Prayer*) indicate a change in emphasis, from reasoned argument to the greater tentativeness and subjectivity that 'reflections' and 'letters' imply.

This shift is apparent also in Lewis's fiction of the 1950s. It becomes more imaginative and mythical, beginning with the seven Chronicles of Narnia, the best-known and most influential of his writings. The Chronicles have been successful because of the atmosphere of their fantasy world, Narnia, as an immensely appealing, idyllic, pastoral land populated with talking animals and made-up creatures like Dufflepuds and Marsh-wiggles, and because of the exciting, suspense-filled adventures that occur in it. The stories unite the Romance genre's emphasis on brave knights, courteous behaviour and heroic courage with the magical world of fairy tales, including their broad, clear-cut themes contrasting good and evil. The Chronicles' use of archetypal plot motifs, character types and symbols adds depth and universality by relating them to the rest of literature and involving them in matters of ultimate concern to all people. Lewis draws these various elements into a unique and appealing combination of adventure, charm and numinousness in plot, characters and theme. At their very best, as for example in the final pages of *The Voyage of the 'Dawn Treader'* and in the final chapter of *The Last Battle*, the Chronicles are high myth, communicating so directly to the imagination through powerful images and symbols that they cannot be translated fully into intellectual terms.

Till We Have Faces: A Myth Retold (1956), Lewis's last work of fiction and the one he considered his best, rises to an even higher level of imaginativeness.[48] It is wholly a work of mythic imagination. The book is a retelling of the Cupid and Psyche myth, from the

Metamorphoses, or *The Golden Ass,* of Lucius Apuleius, a story that had fascinated Lewis since he first read it in 1916. *Till We Have Faces* uses a first-person, unreliable narrator, Psyche's older sister Orual, who writes the book as a defence of her own actions, accusing the gods of treating her unfairly. Orual writes what she believes to be an accurate, truthful account of her life. It is up to the reader to recognize her faults and self-deceptions, without a reliable narrator's help.

A key theme in her story is the tension between head and heart, between reason and spiritual perception. Her tutor (and later advisor), the Fox, is a Stoic, attempting like Lewis's tutor Kirkpatrick to be a totally rational person (he is representative of the spirit of the Greeks and of the Enlightenment). Opposed to him are the Priest of Ungit, on the one hand, with his appreciation of a dark, mysterious holiness, and Psyche, on the other, with her natural, intuitive response to the divine. Orual, as the Fox's student, attempts to follow him and to reject the gods. She must learn that only through the numinous, through that which is beyond reason, can a relationship with the divine begin and her full selfhood be achieved.

Till We Have Faces is a deeply Christian book but in a very different way from Lewis's works in the 1940s. It does not have the clear answers and tidy packaging of the apologetic books, or the allegorical and expository explicitness of *The Pilgrim's Regress* and the Ransom trilogy. It continues the reliance on myth begun in the Chronicles, recognizing the impossibility of spelling out truths intellectually. In earlier works the reason and the imagination were addressed separately – story for the imagination, explanation for the reason. In *Till We Have Faces* that distinction and separation break down and Lewis writes for the whole person, emphasizing not answers and formulas but struggles and the ultimate goal. 'What happens, then, in *Till We Have Faces,*' Gunnar Urang points out, 'is that C. S. Lewis moves toward coming to terms with his own dividedness.'[49] The result is a presentation through myth of the essential Christian experience: one is given a 'taste' of Reality via the story of Orual's achievement of wholeness of self through a right relationship with God. In *Till We Have Faces* in the 1950s, Lewis achieves what he had sought since the 1920s: a full reconciliation and unification of the reason he admired with the imagination he loved.

Notes

1 Margaret E. Rose to C. S. Lewis, 28 May 1962, in *The Collected Letters of C. S. Lewis*, ed. Walter Hooper ([San Francisco]: HarperSanFrancisco, 2007), vol. 3, p. 1346 n. 86.

2 C. S. Lewis to Margaret E. Rose, 30 May 1962, in Lewis, *Collected Letters*, vol. 3, pp. 1346–7.

3 C. S. Lewis, *Surprised by Joy: The Shape of My Early Life* (New York: Harcourt, Brace and World, 1955), pp. 15, 82. Hereafter cited within the text.

4 J. R. R. Tolkien, 'On Fairy-Stories', in *Essays Presented to Charles Williams*, ed. C. S. Lewis (London: Oxford University Press, 1947), p. 66.

5 C. S. Lewis, *An Experiment in Criticism* (Cambridge: Cambridge University Press, 1961), p. 53.

6 C. S. Lewis to Arthur Greeves, 14 March 1916, in Lewis, *Collected Letters*, vol. 1, p. 174.

7 C. S. Lewis to Arthur Greeves, 18 October 1931, in Lewis, *Collected Letters*, vol. 1, p. 977.

8 C. S. Lewis, 'Reason', in C. S. Lewis, *Poems*, ed. Walter Hooper (London: Geoffrey Bles, 1964), p. 81.

9 Owen Barfield, 'C. S. Lewis' (1964), in *Owen Barfield on C. S. Lewis*, ed. G. B. Tennyson (Middletown, CT: Wesleyan University Press, 1989), pp. 5–6.

10 Owen Barfield, *Poetic Diction: A Study in Meaning* (London: Faber and Gwyer, 1928); I. A. Richards, *Principles of Literary Criticism* (London: Kegan Paul, 1925).

11 Lewis, *Collected Letters*, vol. 3, pp. 1600–45.

12 Stephen Thorson, 'Knowing and Being in C. S. Lewis's "Great War" with Owen Barfield', *The Bulletin of the New York C. S. Lewis Society* 15, no. 1 (November 1983), pp. 1–8; '"Knowledge" in C. S. Lewis's Post-Conversion Thought: His Epistemological Method', *Seven: An Anglo-American Literary Review* 9 (1988), pp. 91–116; 'Lewis and Barfield on Imagination', Part 1, *Mythlore* 17, no. 2 (Winter 1990), pp. 12–18, 32; Part 2, *Mythlore* 17, no. 3 (Spring 1991), pp. 16–21; and 'Barfield's Evolution of Consciousness: How Much Did Lewis Accept?' *Seven: An Anglo-American Literary Review* 15 (1998), pp. 9–35.

13 Barfield, 'Lewis, Truth and Imagination' (1978), in Tennyson, *Owen Barfield on C. S. Lewis*, p. 97.

14 Thorson, 'Lewis and Barfield on Imagination', Part 1, p. 15.

15 Thorson, 'Knowing and Being', p. 5.

16 Thorson, 'Lewis and Barfield on Imagination', Part 2, p. 18.

17 C. S. Lewis, *Mere Christianity* (London: Geoffrey Bles, 1952), p. 23.

18 Lewis, *Mere Christianity*, p. 24.

19 Lewis, *Mere Christianity*, p. 44.

20 C. S. Lewis to Arthur Greeves, 18 October 1931, in Lewis, *Collected Letters*, vol. 1, p. 976.

21 C. S. Lewis to Arthur Greeves, 18 October 1931, in Lewis, *Collected Letters*, vol. 1, pp. 976–7.

22 C. S. Lewis to Dom Bede Griffiths, 24 April 1936, in Lewis, *Collected Letters*, vol. 2, p. 189.

23 C. S. Lewis, 'Religion: Reality or Substitute?' (1941), in *Christian Reflections*, ed. Walter Hooper (Grand Rapids, MI: Eerdmans, 1967), p. 43.

24 C. S. Lewis to Mary Van Deusen, 14 July 1951, in Lewis, *Collected Letters*, vol. 3, p. 129.

25 C. S. Lewis, 'Bluspels and Flalansferes: A Semantic Nightmare' (1939), in *Selected Literary Essays*, ed. Walter Hooper (Cambridge: Cambridge University Press, 1969), p. 265.

26 C. S. Lewis, 'Man or Rabbit?' (1946?), in *God in the Dock: Essays on Theology and Ethics*, ed. Walter Hooper (Grand Rapids, MI: Eerdmans, 1970), p. 108.

27 Lewis, 'Religion: Reality or Substitute?', p. 41.

28 C. S. Lewis, *The Four Loves* (London: Geoffrey Bles, 1960), p. 143.

29 C. S. Lewis, 'Myth Became Fact' (1944), in *God in the Dock*, p. 65.

30 Charlie W. Starr, 'Meaning, Meanings, and Epistemology in C. S. Lewis', *Mythlore* 25, no. 3/4 (Spring/Summer 2007), pp. 164, 165.

31 Lewis, 'Myth Became Fact', pp. 65–6.

32 Lewis, 'Bluspels and Flalansferes', p. 254.

33 Starr, 'Meaning, Meanings, and Epistemology', p. 177.

34 Lewis, *An Experiment in Criticism*, p. 139.

35 Lewis, *An Experiment in Criticism*, p. 141.

36 Lewis, 'Myth Became Fact', p. 66.

37 Lewis, 'Myth Became Fact', p. 66.

38 C. S. Lewis, 'The Language of Religion', in *Christian Reflections*, p. 136.

39 C. S. Lewis, *The Great Divorce* (London: Geoffrey Bles, 1945), p. 41.

40 Lewis, 'Myth Became Fact', p. 66.

41 Starr, 'Meaning, Meanings, and Epistemology', p. 176.

42 C. S. Lewis, *The Problem of Pain* (London: Centenary, 1940), p. 81.

43 C. S. Lewis to Dom Bede Griffiths, 23 May 1936, in Lewis, *Collected Letters*, vol. 2, p. 192.

44 C. S. Lewis to Dom Bede Griffiths, 23 May 1936, in Lewis, *Collected Letters*, vol. 2, p. 193.

45 Lewis, 'Bluspels and Flalansferes', p. 257.

46 C. S. Lewis to Dom Bede Griffiths, 23 May 1936, in Lewis, *Collected Letters*, vol. 2, p. 191.

47 C. S. Lewis to Sister Penelope CSMV, 9 July [August] 1939, in Lewis, *Collected Letters*, vol. 2, p. 262.
48 C. S. Lewis to Anne and Martin Kilmer, 7 August 1957, in Lewis, *Collected Letters*, vol. 3, p. 873.
49 Gunnar Urang, *Shadows of Heaven: Religion and Fantasy in the Writing of C. S. Lewis, Charles Williams, and J. R. R. Tolkien* (Philadelphia: Pilgrim, 1971), p. 49.

Figure 2 Austin Farrer in the 1960s.
Used with the kind permission of the Trustees of the K. D. Farrer Trust and
with permission of Caroline Farrer and Nick Newton.

2

Austin Farrer: The sacramental imagination

EDWARD HENDERSON

Lewis and his fiction-writing friends use imagination to explore the ways Christian truth can be lived – and refused – in all manners and circumstances of life. Austin Farrer, on the other hand, wrote no fiction, but his philosophy, theology and biblical scholarship make clear that imagination is at the centre of Christian faith. More than a way of presenting the faith, the master images of Christianity make up the very form of understanding by which God makes God's Self known; it is through these images that Christian faith exists.

Farrer does more than point to the role of imagination in divine revelation. He brings faith and reason together by enabling us to see how the biblically imagined life is not a blind and irrational life of faith against reason but a fulfilment of reason's 'supreme exercise', the effort to know 'what is most worthy of love, and most binding on conduct, in the world of real existence'.[1] This highest and noblest aim of reason is realized in the life that engages with God through the great images of the Old and New Testaments that make up the Christian story. The images shape life as engagement with God. Living by the images, persons can hope to know God's active presence as they are made more truly themselves by being made more truly lovers of God and neighbour.

Wherever we look we see the centrality of imagination in faith. Stories of persons and events are charged with God's presence: Adam, Eve, Abraham, Israel, Joseph, Moses, David, Jesus, Mary, covenant, Passover, exodus, sacrificial lamb, expiation, atonement, dying and rising, kingdom of God, suffering servant, messiah, king, body of Christ, New Jerusalem. These persons and events belong in the long history of a people's effort to know and to live in community with

God. They are not bare facts, each one locked within itself in its own time and place; they are images, ways of seeing persons and events in terms of other persons and events, ways of knowing what God has done and is doing and ways, too, of responding to and engaging with God. When Christians gather to hear the word preached, it is the rich fabric of images that they rehearse and apply. When they baptize and when they celebrate the Holy Supper, they are engaging with God by enacting images.

Take the Supper as an example. The Eucharist, more than any Christian practice, gathers up all the images and expresses the whole story of creation and redemption in a way that incorporates the participants into the story and so begins to move them into a life shaped by the image. Farrer goes so far as to say that the Supper 'is not a special part of our religion, it is just our religion, sacramentally enacted'.[2] The Eucharist sums up the whole of Christ's ministry, crucifixion and resurrection. Here is the Son of Man and Son of God living faithfully in God, dying and rising and bringing into new life those who share his ministry and crucifixion. Here is the kingdom of God, not as a nation-state but as the heavenly kingdom, the reign of God, the New Jerusalem, set in our midst around the rule of sacrificial love lived by one who is Israel, Messiah, King and suffering servant. Here are faithful believers performing the images, nourished by the bread and wine for life among trials and troubles but taking them also as food and drink of new and unending life in the eternal heavenly banquet with Christ.

Farrer, Lewis and Tolkien

In the 1940s, Lewis, Tolkien and Farrer connected in discussing myth and the Christian story of the birth, life, death and resurrection of Christ. In 1944 Lewis published 'Myth Became Fact', in which he presented what he had learned from Owen Barfield and J. R. R. Tolkien.[3] Myths are not 'lies of poets', as Lewis had thought before his conversion;[4] they are works of inspired sub-creators that express significant truth about life and reality. The biblical story can also be called a myth; but it differs from pagan myths, say Lewis and Tolkien, by being written by God in 'words' that were the actual lives of real people in definite places and times, especially Jesus of Nazareth. The Christian myth, in other words, is not primarily the words written in Scripture. It is the lives and actions of persons. These lives and actions are God's message; they tell what God is doing. In the words of the Letter to the Hebrews: 'Long ago God spoke to our ancestors in many and various ways by the prophets, but in these last days he has spoken to us by a Son.'[5] The myth is written in God's speech in flesh and blood. That, both Lewis and Tolkien believed, makes the Christian story a 'fact' of history, not a fictitious expression of human wisdom created by poetic priests and prophets.

A few months after Lewis's 'Myth Became Fact', Farrer presented 'Can Myth Be Fact?' to the Socratic Club, turning Lewis's flat declaration into a question.[6] Farrer did not disagree with Lewis and Tolkien that the primary Christian story is 'written' by God in real lives and events. But more than Lewis and Tolkien, Farrer had the questioning philosopher's mind and needed to satisfy himself that the questions could be answered: What does it mean to say that the Gospel is myth become 'fact'? If, as Lewis and Tolkien believed, the human words that tell the story nourish the soul, does it matter whether the myth is fact? If the myth is indeed fact, how did it become so? What kind of sense does it make to say that God is the author of the story and that God tells it in the real lives of persons and events? Finally, is it reasonable to believe the myth?

In what sense fact?

It would be nonsense to say that the myth is fact if 'fact' means raw and uninterpreted experience, an unambiguous presence given to persons as it is in itself. If philosophers have learned anything in the doomed 300-year quest for a certain, indubitable, incorrigible givenness of truth about reality, it is that there is no uninterpreted experience. Experience always comes interpreted at a variety of levels: by the operations of our sensory organs, by our language and emotions, by our expectations and imaginations. The 'facts' of physics are events interpreted according to a conceptual model of forces, causes and effects in a setting of experimental contrivance. The 'facts' of chemistry are events interpreted according to models of atomic and molecular structures and valences. The 'facts' of psychology are events interpreted according to various theories of human behaviour. Similarly, the 'fact' of Christianity is the event of Jesus of Nazareth interpreted in images that come from the Jewish understanding of

God's actions, will and promises, which developed over centuries of efforts to live in relationship with God.

Farrer insists that the events of Jesus' life – the teaching, even the miracles, the crucifixion and the resurrection – do not by themselves reveal God. The events have to be interpreted as the place of God's active presence, as what God does. They are interpreted so by reference to events already understood as things God has done, is doing or has promised.

> The great images interpreted the events of Christ's ministry, death and resurrection, and the events interpreted the images; the interplay of the two is revelation. Certainly the events without the images would be no revelation at all, and the images without the events would remain shadows on the clouds. The events by themselves are not revelation, for they do not by themselves reveal the divine work which is accomplished in them: the martyrdom of a virtuous Rabbi and his miraculous return are not of themselves the redemption of the world.[7]

Grant, then, that the Christian myth is not fact by being the description of incontestable, given and uninterpreted actions of God. We can say, however, that the myth is 'fact' if it is a true understanding of God's action in real persons and events. That is, the myth is fact in that it is not fiction told about imaginary persons and events. By contrast, the polytheistic myths of the ancient world are fiction, not facts; for example, the story of Athena springing full-grown from the head of Zeus. It is conceivable that the Zeus–Athena story has in its unknown provenance some encounter with actual events, but there is no good reason for thinking that the story describes events involving actual divine agents. The story may express an important kind of truth, but it is not fact in the sense that Christians claim for the myth of Christ.

For the Christian myth to be 'fact' in an acceptable sense of the term, it must meet two conditions: its written or spoken words must be about real persons and occurrences in the world, and the images used to interpret the events must be applied truly to them. In meeting the first condition, understanding necessarily remains at the level of things and events that are part of the created world. But the Christian myth is about what God has done and is doing. To interpret the events of the story as God's action is to see persons and events in the world through images that express the action of God, of God who is creator of the world, not one of its created components. Jesus is the Christ, the Messiah, the Son of Man, the Son of God, the Passover sacrificed for us to deliver us from bondage and into God's kingdom. To believe that the Christian story is true is to believe that the images of God's actions, which were developed in the history of the Jews as they sought to live in relation to God, are truly ascribed to Jesus because they truly represent what God is doing in him.

We cannot know precisely what Jesus himself said and what was attributed to him by the Gospel writers as they tried to express what they came to see as the essence of his life.[8] There is legendary embellishment and distortion; the Gospel writers write from their own perspectives to express their theological understanding.[9] Nevertheless, Farrer argues, the Jewish images used by the Gospel writers are the same as the images that surely provided the content of Jesus' mind.[10] Therefore, it is unreasonable to suppose that all the images that express divine presence were overlaid by the biblical writers on actions of Jesus that were in no way mediated by those same Jewish images: 'from a purely secular point of view, there is no superiority in the common hypothesis that the transformation took place first in the minds of the disciples and was projected back upon him'.[11] It is more reasonable to believe that Jesus himself would have thought and lived through the images of his faith. But no purely historical evidence exists that could establish the truth of the images that express divine action in historical events. Belief in the active presence of God in mundane events can never be proved solely by the occurrence of particular events but must be affirmed, Farrer says, 'only by faith'.[12]

The words 'only by faith' are liable to be grossly misunderstood. They do not mean to believe by 'a blind and irrational decision about something that either lacks sufficient evidence or contradicts existing evidence'. Rather, what Farrer means by 'faith' is a way of life. Christian faith is a way of life the content and exercise of which have the form of a trusting and obedient engagement with God. Faith's understanding, which is given and carried in the images, is not believed because its meaning lies before us as bare, inert and uninterpreted facts or even as facts interpreted by historical methods. Christians believe the myth because it effectively mediates their existence in the world. As they structure their lives by it, they find themselves engaged with the living God and their efforts to know 'what is most worthy of love, and most binding on conduct' satisfied.

Why need myth be fact?

Lewis was especially interested in myths of dying and rising gods, for they resemble the Christian story of the dying and rising Christ. He wrote of the pagan myths in *Miracles* and made the pattern the basis of his retelling of the myth of Cupid and Psyche in *Till We Have Faces*. But if the pagan myths are fiction, even profoundly wise fiction, why should it matter whether the Christian myth is fact instead of fiction? Lewis's own work in writing religiously charged fiction suggests that it is the symbolic meaning that counts, not the rootedness of the myth in history. And in 'Myth Became Fact' he expresses the conviction that 'A man who disbelieved the Christian story as fact but continually fed on it as myth would perhaps be more spiritually alive than one who assented and did not think much about it. . . . The poor man may be clinging (with a wisdom he himself by no means understands) to that which is his life . . .'[13] Farrer recognizes the truth of Lewis's claim, but he wonders why, if myth nourishes just by being a good story, it should be important for the Christian myth to have historical roots. Why not just let the story be a story and not worry about its connections with the real events and persons of history? It is clear, of course, that Lewis did think it important for the myth to be 'fact', but he does not tell us why. Farrer, on the other hand, offers an explanation.

Even if one believes in the reality of one transcendent God and even if one holds that God inspired the Gospel writers to see and express profound truths through fiction, such interpretations, by reducing the story to inspired wise fiction, leave humankind on its own. They recognize wisdom in the story, but they put all the weight on people to understand and act on that wisdom. If that were all, then there would be no need for God. God would be a character in the story, but not a living God who actually engages people. It is a short step from here to what Farrer calls 'pious atheism', according to which God is a fictitious character in the same way Zeus, Odin and Ra are fictitious characters in pagan myths.[14]

If the story has not been enacted by God among people in a particular place and time, it is like a story parents might tell their children about an imaginary village in which people could live in happiness if they would make the village real. The village remains a vision of the possible. Such a story might include directives and morals about how life could be lived so as to get the village started and about what life would be like if people did get it going and actually lived by the story's wisdom. But it is only a wise story about an imagined village, not an introduction into the actual life of a real village. Even if the story were inspired by God, as one might believe God inspired Shakespeare in the writing of plays, it would leave the divinely inspired story of the kingdom still the story of an imaginary kingdom and its establishment entirely up to human enactment.

But if the myth is 'fact', if the story of God's kingdom is told in actual people and events, then God 'came among them, bringing his kingdom . . . He set the divine life in human neighbourhood . . .'[15] That is, God does not only inspire humankind to have ideas about the kingdom; God enacts the kingdom: God gets it going and, by enacting it, 'sets us in motion'.[16] The events would mean nothing to us – could not be known as the actions of God – without the mythic images through which we understand what they are. They could not even be the enactment of the kingdom if they were not actions through which God seeks to engage us in a life with God. But the story of the kingdom is not only a story; it is made a real kingdom by being told in real events. To encounter the story as fact is to encounter God in action and to have the possibility of response.

That is what faith is: responding in loving and trusting obedience to the divine life of creating, redeeming and perfecting. Inasmuch as the faithful response is intended and enacted through the images and the understanding they give, the images mediate the Christian's engagement with God. They are sacramental. Shaping the faithful response, they are the outward and visible expression of God's inward and gracious action.

How did the myth become fact?

How is it possible for the story to have become fact in the events of Israel's history and of Jesus' life? Farrer makes a brief beginning of an answer in 'Can Myth Be Fact?' by recalling just one strand of biblical imagery: the image of the Son of Man. The essay is followed by *The Glass of Vision*, in which he develops his thought about the role of images in a discussion of the relationships between Scripture, poetry and metaphysics. There follow a number of books of biblical interpretation, short essays and sermons in which Farrer complicates and applies this emphasis on Scripture as inspired literature. He stresses the ongoing interpretation and reinterpretation of events, persons and actions in terms of the core images that mediate the recognition of God's action. Take the discussion in 'Can Myth Be Fact?' as a first explanatory example.

Farrer connects the Son of Man with the story of Adam in Genesis and turns to Daniel's use of the story, a use provoked by the experience of exile along with belief in the creation story and the covenantal promises of God. The prophetic author was committed to the promises of the covenant, yet found Israel still struggling in captivity. Farrer reads Daniel's vision as one according to which Israel is living in the fifth day of creation, the day when the monsters are brought forth from the deep, the day when beasts reign instead of the Son of Man, instead of the man created in the divine image to rule over the earth by living in faithful relation with God. When, the prophet wondered, would the purpose of God for Israel and humankind be realized? 'When would he put down the beast and enthrone the Son of Man, the Man in the image of God?'[17] In his vision Daniel sees one like a Son of Man coming to the creator and being given 'dominion and glory and kingship . . . that shall never be destroyed'.[18] The vision expresses Daniel's hope and belief that God will indeed bring to fulfilment the intention of creation, which had been frustrated by human infidelity. His hope and belief are about what God will do, but are a hope and a belief possible only through images from Scripture, images that express God's action of creating and redeeming. God's action can only be thought with the help of imagination, which connects the present circumstances and hopes for future life with stories from Scripture and tradition.

So much, then, for the way the exilic prophet uses the ancient myth. Farrer argues that Jesus of Nazareth fulfils the hope of Daniel's prophetic vision by living the scriptural images in a relationship of loving and obedient trust in God. He recounts Mark's story of Christ in the High Priest's court where Jesus makes his identity as the Son of God 'the issue upon which he wills to die'.[19] Here Jesus accepts the title of 'Christ' and interprets the images in terms that recall Daniel's vision: he will reign in glory. For Jesus to say so in the circumstances seems insanity. But Jesus has in his life and ministry already taken to himself more of the Adamic story than that Adam was created to rule. He has also taken to himself that part of the story according to which Adam was naked and cast out, ploughing among thistles in the wilderness. Jesus has taken to himself the whole experience of fallen humankind: with the beasts, tempted by the enemy, yet renouncing the offer to be God to himself. Instead of falling, Jesus stands, founds a new humankind in the group of 12 apostles, forgives sins on earth, claims jurisdiction over the Sabbath and, renouncing the kind of power exercised by fallen humankind, instead enacts the power of God in trusting and obedient suffering. So the myth became fact by 'the slow formation of the perfect, the typical myth of Adam: its taking up and projection into the future by such prophets as him we call Daniel; its acceptance by Jesus as the meaning of his destiny, so that he sets out to be the new Adam, the Son of Man'.[20]

Another example of the same kind of interpretation can be found in *The Triple Victory*, a Lent book for the Archbishop of Canterbury in 1965. There Farrer draws on his study of the Gospel according to St Matthew to explain how Matthew's account of the temptations of Christ in the wilderness uses the Old Testament's matrix of images to present Jesus and the theological meaning of his life. Here Jesus is a new Moses in the wilderness, and at the same time he is the Children of Israel, experiencing the temptations they faced in the wilderness but overcoming them. We do not know whether Jesus himself described his experience to his disciples or whether it is 'St Matthew's dramatization in a single scene of trials which beset Jesus throughout his ministry'.[21] But we are well within the rights of reason to believe that in the combination of the great images and the actions of Jesus' ministry, 'we have the mind of Christ'.[22] He did not, of course, think of himself in terms of the Nicene Creed: 'God from God, Light from Light, true God from true God, begotten not made, of one being with the Father'. These words may apply truly, but they represent the wisdom of a later generation, not the way Christ could have thought about himself. But Son of Man, Son of God, Israel, Messiah, King and Lord – these terms and the rich stories behind them form the principal content of a 'web of interacting minds' of which Jesus was one and on which Jesus' life made a decisive impact.[23] The core images formed the deep grammar of Jesus' faith, so that even if he did not explicitly apply all the images to himself, Farrer suggests, they so mediated his life in the world of his time that he knew 'how to be the Son of God' by living them.[24]

Bringing the images together as Christ did in his life utterly transformed their meaning. A crucified king differs vastly from a messiah and king who is a head of state backed by political and military power. The new religion of Christianity was born when Jesus lived the old images, breaking them on the hard rocks of reality and giving them a new meaning. The process of transforming the images began before Christ. The people of Israel outgrew their literal meaning; for example, they outgrew the expectation that if they would be good, God would always defend and reward them with worldly blessings. 'But their prophets did not dismiss the images of covenant and kingdom as meaningless: they adhered to the promises expressed in the images and in that national crucifixion they crucified the literal sense of the promises in order that God might reveal to them the true and spiritual sense.'[25] Even more, Christ

> did not take the promises of God to be a jest, because they could not be literally fulfilled. He did not say 'In the face of Roman power we can found no messianic kingdom here.' He said: 'In the face of Roman power we will see what sort of messianic kingdom God will make.' He kept the words and God changed the thing, and so we still call him Christ, Messiah, King, but not in the pre-crucifixion sense.[26]

That Jesus took the images to himself and lived according to them in loving and faithful obedience, however, does not in itself make the ascription of the images to him true. Jesus could have been deluded; so also could the Gospel writers have been. For the images to be true of Jesus, God had to be present and acting in him so as to continue the story beyond what Jesus had so far lived. God had to 'bend and shape historical fact by that control which is his alone into the expressive completion of the redeeming mystery . . . [by raising] Jesus from the dead, and enthron[ing] the Son of Man at the right hand of Almighty Power, so that the divine image might reign in a kingdom both of Man and God, through the union of redeemed men with the enthroned Christ'.[27]

How can that be, and on what grounds can we believe it?

How can God be the author?

Tolkien, Lewis and Farrer agree that the events of Christ's life, death and resurrection are a 'myth', a 'story', told by God. We have seen that this means that it is God who has enacted the Christian story. But if God 'wrote' the story, how can the actors and actions in which God wrote it be real? More specifically, how can a man acting freely and as himself be at the same time the action of God? Some have believed that the biblical characters were puppets and God a puppeteer, but it is foolish to think that Jesus lacked the integrity and freedom of a fully human person. What would be the point of calling him obedient, loving, faithful, the new and unfallen Adam if he were some 'divinely mesmerized sleepwalker' or 'a jointed doll pulled by heavenly wires'?[28] No. Christ is real, and he is free. 'Never', says Farrer, 'was there a man whose words and actions were more utterly his own. . . . the sacrifice on which he spent his blood was a decision personally made in agonies of sweat.'[29] How, then, can Christ's life be his own and at the same time be a story written by God?

Farrer answers this question with the idea of 'double agency', which is the idea that God acts in the actions of creatures and does so most obviously in those actions in which persons are faithfully obedient to God's will, God acting in the actions of creatures but always in a way that lets them retain their integrity as real beings rather than in a way that overrides or cancels their real being. Farrer sees the life of Jesus as the paradigm case of double agency: 'If any man made his own life, Jesus did. Yet what was the impression he left on his friends? That his whole life was the pure and simple act of God. What Jesus did was simply what God did to save us all.'[30]

It may be paradoxical to say that the life of Christ is both his own and God acting in him, but it is not contradictory. For God is unique, not one constituent of the world competing with other constituents in exerting energy that transfers from one thing to another, but the source and reason-why of the world and all its constituents. Therefore we can say without contradiction that God acts in creatures with an action that does not cancel the creature but lets it be itself. We see it with greatest clarity in Jesus and in saintly lives, but we may also experience it in our own lives when we act in faithful and loving obedience to God. For then it is that we find both that there is more than ourselves acting and that we are more truly and fully ourselves as a result. 'Double agency' is a term that designates a phenomenon we recognize from our own experience, but it is not an explanation of how God does it any more than quantum physics is an explanation of how a particle can have either its position or its velocity known but not both.

Farrer shared with Dorothy L. Sayers the parable of the divine novelist or divine playwright as a parable of double agency. God, he says, is not like the bad novelist or playwright who forces the story on the characters but like the good novelist who lets the characters develop naturally, or like the playwright who gets the actors on the stage and gets the play out of them by letting them be themselves.[31]

Farrer extended the idea of double agency to cover the whole field of revelation in Scripture and beyond. As ancient persons sought to know 'what is most worthy of love, and most binding on conduct', God acted in their creative imaginations, and they brought forth images of God and of God's will. Through the 'hard rocks' of historical circumstance and event, the images were refined.[32] Confusions and errors persisted, not only historical and scientific errors but also theological errors. Nevertheless, God acts in and through human actions and in human understanding, even when persons are disobedient and confused: 'divine power being as much shown in overcoming the weakness of its instruments, as it is shown in shaping them to its purpose'.[33]

So it is that believers can affirm that God has acted in the history of Israel, in the minds of scribe, priest and prophet, in the life of Jesus and in the Church, to tell truths about what is most worth loving and what loving requires persons to do. More than this, believers can affirm that this God does not leave humankind on its own but acts in the world to engage and transform.

Can reason believe the myth?

Is it reasonable to believe the Christian story, to believe that as a story told in human words it not only presents a wise vision for life but truly presents what God has done and is doing and provides a way for persons to engage with the living God? There is no question of proving the story in the way demanded by scientific rationality, although Farrer believed that its rootedness in history, in actual persons and events, is well substantiated. Even so, this fact does not guarantee the truth of the story's images, for they assert the action and presence of God: that Jesus of Nazareth is Son of Man, Son of God, the Christ, the Lamb of God, our Passover, our Saviour and King; that Jesus was not only crucified but also raised; that he ascended to the Father; and that he lives in the Father's presence as human person taken into divine life and as one with whom, by the power of the Holy Spirit, we can be engaged in an unending saving relationship that will culminate in the fulfilment and perfection of all Creation.

Can we rationally believe that this image-filled story, this myth, presents real actions of God in events in the world and that in this sense myth is fact? Farrer's answer takes us into his philosophy, where he sees two components as fundamental in human knowing: activity and imagination. All knowing derives from acting in the world and undergoing the effects the world has on us because of the way we act in it. What we know depends upon what we do. But what we do depends on the images that direct the doing; they make our action what it is, and, consequently, they shape the way we are affected by the world we encounter.[34]

Why images? Why not ideas or concepts? Because, Farrer thought, images are always at the bottom of even the most abstract thought. Imagination cannot be separated from reason. For example, if we think of the wisdom about human nature that has been delivered through the ages by religion, by philosophy and literature and by the sciences, we see that it is carried in images. What is a human being? The image and child of God, say the Jewish Scriptures; a mixture of the blood of Kingu with the flesh of Ea, says the Babylonian story of Marduk; a god-like immortal soul, says Plato; a rational animal, says Aristotle; an angel, says Dante; a system of minute particles acting on each other by external and coercive causation, say physics and chemistry; a DNA-directed, biochemical organism, says biology; a computer made of meat, say some cognitive scientists; and so on and on it goes, from discipline to discipline, school to school. These are all images or models. Some use the tool of mathematics to make their models unambiguous, but even measurement is an application of imagination, for it sees its objects by analogy with the relations numbers have to other numbers. The sciences make much of experimental testing, but even experimental testing does not remove science from the realm of imagination: experimentation is a matter of tinkering with the world in model-directed ways.[35]

That reason works with imagination does not mean that imagination-mediated knowing is false or that it creates the reality it knows. It means that reality is never known simply as it is in itself but always as it affects us. We are not objective observers of reality; we are messily immersed in it. Knocking about in the world, we undergo its effects as it qualifies those special activities called senses, which are themselves ways of acting that let us be affected in standard ways by what is encountered. As we modify our activity with the help of language and the imagining that language makes possible, we undergo further effects of the world. Reality reveals itself as multi-faceted. It affects our different modes of activity in different ways and so lets us know its various facets: treating bodies through bio-chemical and physiological models, we are able to know diseases and methods of sustaining and restoring health; treating bodies as the bodies of persons, we are able to know friends.

The Christian myth, however, is not a simple image about a limited facet of reality. It is a comprehensive map of reality taken as the sphere of human life in which persons are concerned to know what is ultimately most important: 'what is most worthy of love, and most binding on conduct'. So understood, the myth is not an entertaining story, not even an edifying story expressing inspired wisdom and illustrating high moral principles. The Christian story told by God in lived images answers the ultimate questions that reason asks, and it answers them in a way that addresses – indeed, that confronts – persons with an unconditional claim on their lives. It says that the highest and best possibility for human life is for persons to be taken into the life of God. What is most worthy of love? It is God, trinity of persons in unity of being, abyss of ongoing active love, love perfectly given, perfectly received, perfectly returned and perfectly shared. What is most binding on conduct? It is the will of God. And the will of God, revealed by God's action in Christ, is that persons join themselves to Christ's life by obediently and trustingly entering into the unconditional love of God and neighbours, crucifixion in the hope of resurrection.

If imagination cannot be separated from reasoning, then neither can it be separated from living. The Christian myth is not, we have said, primarily the story's human words. It is, as Farrer, Lewis and Tolkien have agreed, the story that is the life and person of Jesus Christ. The living myth, therefore, is the action of God confronting persons and claiming their lives in response. When persons make the response, they are joining their lives to the eternal creating and redeeming action of God, and the images through which persons engage with God become the means whereby God's gracious action takes visible effect in the world. The images mediate the interaction of God and persons. They become sacraments, as, indeed, has been long recognized in the image-shaped actions of baptism and Eucharist.

Is it reasonable to believe that the myth is true, that it is an action of God now going on? It is if one is willing to feel the full impact of its total and unconditional claim on life, for there is where the ultimate questions of the truth-seeking intelligence are answered.[36] There is no possibility for the story to be proved true as a theory about reality. It can only be proved in the life that responds to the demands it makes. There is a long history of persons who have entered into life through the story and who have found in doing so that God has taken their lives into the divine life, accomplishing in them what they could not do for themselves, transforming them into persons who more truly love God and their neighbours and making them more truly themselves. The Church in its many manifestations helps by enacting the images in ways that incorporate persons into the myth that is fact and gets them moving in the life of Christ by the power of the Holy Spirit.

> There is no shortcut to the understanding of God's promises. You cannot do it by the wisdom of this world, or by logical sleight of hand. You can do it by active faith alone, by believing in God who has promised, by persevering in purity of life, in constant prayer, in Christ's sacraments, in obedience to every showing of God's will. Then God will reveal to you his excellent things. For, says Christ's Apostle, when in the wisdom of God the world failed by wisdom to know God, it pleased God by the folly of the gospel to save believers.[37]

Farrer did not hope to satisfy the philosophers that the rationality of faith is superior to that of philosophy and science. But for those willing to consider the possibility, he made clear how believing and acting the Christian story is a realization of reason's supreme goal: to know 'what is most worthy of love, and most binding on conduct'. Believing the myth takes reason beyond what reason can know with certainty. The story's truth will not be known with finality until we dance the dance of faith in the kingdom of God. But, says Farrer with Lewis and friends, the dance has begun, and we are invited to join in.

Notes

1 Austin Farrer, *The End of Man*, ed. Charles C. Conti (London: SPCK, 1973), p. 157.

2 Austin Farrer, *The Crown of the Year: Weekly Paragraphs for the Holy Sacrament* (London: Dacre, 1952), p. 58.

3 C. S. Lewis, 'Myth Became Fact' (1944), in *God in the Dock: Essays on Theology and Ethics*, ed. Walter Hooper (Grand Rapids, MI: Eerdmans, 1970), pp. 63–7.

4 Humphrey Carpenter, *The Inklings: C. S. Lewis, J. R. R. Tolkien, Charles Williams and Their Friends* (1978; repr., London: HarperCollins, 2006), ch. 3.

5 Hebrews 1.1–2a.

6 Austin Farrer, 'Can Myth be Fact?' (1945), in *Interpretation and Belief*, ed. Charles C. Conti (London: SPCK, 1976), pp. 165–75.

7 Austin Farrer, *The Glass of Vision* (London: Dacre, 1948), p. 43.

8 Austin Farrer, *A Rebirth of Images: The Making of St John's Apocalypse* (London: Dacre, 1949), p. 16.

9 Austin Farrer, *Saving Belief: A Discussion of Essentials* (1964; repr., Harrisburg, PA: Mowbray, 1994), p. 59.

10 Farrer, *Saving Belief*, p. 66.

11 Farrer, *Rebirth of Images*, p. 14.

12 Farrer, 'Can Myth be Fact?', p. 175.

13 Lewis, 'Myth Became Fact', p. 67.

14 Austin Farrer, *Faith and Speculation* (New York: New York University Press, 1967), p. 48.

15 Farrer, *Saving Belief*, p. 99.

16 Farrer, *Saving Belief*, p. 105.

17 Farrer, 'Can Myth be Fact?', p. 172.

18 Daniel 7.14.

19 Farrer, 'Can Myth be Fact?', p. 173.

20 Farrer, 'Can Myth be Fact?', p. 174.

21 Austin Farrer, *The Triple Victory: Christ's Temptations according to St Matthew* (London: Faith Press, 1965), p. 14.

22 1 Corinthians 2.16; quoted in Austin Farrer, 'A University Sermon', presented in 1948 as The Hulsean Sermon and printed in Philip Curtis, *A Hawk Among Sparrows: A Biography of Austin Farrer* (London: SPCK, 1985), p. 238.

23 Farrer, 'A University Sermon', p. 238.

24 Farrer, *Interpretation and Belief*, p. 135.
25 Austin Farrer, *Austin Farrer: The Essential Sermons*, ed. Leslie Houlden (London: SPCK, 1991), p. 119.
26 Farrer, *Essential Sermons*, p. 119.
27 Farrer, 'Can Myth be Fact?', p. 175.
28 Farrer, *Essential Sermons*, p. 138.
29 Farrer, *Essential Sermons*, p. 138.
30 Farrer, *Essential Sermons*, p. 138.
31 Dorothy L. Sayers, *The Mind of the Maker* (1941; repr., San Francisco: HarperSanFrancisco, 1987), ch. 5; Austin Farrer, *Reflective Faith: Essays in Philosophical Theology*, ed. Charles C. Conti (London: SPCK, 1972), pp. 179–83.
32 Farrer, *Rebirth of Images*, pp. 13–14.
33 Farrer, *Faith and Speculation*, p. 103.
34 Austin Farrer, *Finite and Infinite: A Philosophical Essay* (2nd edn; London: Dacre, 1959), ch. 20, and *Faith and Speculation*, chs 1–4.
35 Farrer, *Glass of Vision*, pp. 64–8.
36 Farrer, *Interpretation and Belief*, p. 5.
37 Farrer, *Essential Sermons*, p. 120.

Figure 3 Dorothy L. Sayers.
National Portrait Gallery, London.

3

Dorothy L. Sayers: War and redemption

ANN LOADES

Dorothy L. Sayers came to maturity during the First World War and lived through the eventful responses to it of the 1920s and 1930s, responses that led almost inevitably to the turmoil and disasters of the Second. More directly and intentionally than C. S. Lewis and the other friends who shared these times and stared with her at the possible collapse of European society, she came to see her most pressing call to be helping her nation move beyond the wars and their consequences. She believed that recovery required society to become more just and that it could become so only by reappropriating basic Christian beliefs: creation, Incarnation, Trinity, sin, Atonement. These dogmas teach us the truth about ourselves and God; consequently, they show us how we can live in the 'city' more justly than had been done in the years leading up to and including the two world wars.

The dogmas are not abstract principles; they find their meaning in life. When rightly held, they are at work directing the drama of the soul's choice. The doctrines must be shown, presented, made visible, so that persons can grab hold of them and give them root. Thus, she has the choir in her 1946 play, *The Just Vengeance*, pray for God to

> Throw open the gate, throw
> Open the gate, show
> The image of truth in the place of the images, show,
> Show![1]

Dorothy L. Sayers takes us to 'the place of the images' and shows us the truth of faith as it can be lived in our fallen world.[2] To do this she works in an amazing range of genres – from advertising to detective fiction, literary criticism, poetry, plays for theatre and for performance in cathedrals, theology, personal and social ethics, reviews, broadcasting, autobiography, letter-writing, lecturing, translation and commentary on texts. In all these forms her conviction that we relate to God through fictional, poetic, dramatic, biblical and creedal images stands out in bold relief. Thus we find her exploring the 'liveability' of Christian doctrine even in her detective novels.

Sayers became more intentional about showing the images when in the late 1930s she began to write plays in which she could literally get doctrine on stage. Her most important theological essay, *The Mind of the Maker*, also stresses the point that we can know God because we are created in the image of God. That she gave the last decade of her life to translating and commenting on Dante's *Divine Comedy* also underlines the emphasis on images, for, inspired by Charles Williams, she saw Dante as the great poet of the way of affirmation, of knowing God through the images of God.

Preparation

Sayers was born in 1893 toward the end of the Victorian era, the only child of well-educated parents. Her father was headmaster of the school that educated the boys who sang in the choir of Christ Church, Oxford (the diocesan cathedral as well as part of the University of Oxford), and there she was baptized. From her earliest years, her mother had her carried down to her bedroom, where she read aloud to her each morning; Dorothy was reading before she was four years old. When she was but six, her father began the study of Latin with her, at which she might have done better had she been able to hold conversations in it, as she could in French and German. She also became a good violinist, but her skill was primarily with words; she was likely to remember almost anything repeated to her in verse. Thus far, her education was patterned largely on that of her mother and her mother's contemporaries; but new opportunities for girls had become apparent, not least to parents who had observed them at close hand in Oxford.

The long Western tradition that asserted women's intellectual inferiority took time to erode; and, indeed, Sayers was to erode it in her own person in various ways, including the publication of polemical essays. One, entitled 'Are Women Human?' (1938), was an address originally written for a women's society and directly addressed to her own Church of England. Another, 'The Human-Not-Quite-Human' (1941), was a criticism of the legacy of defective Christian anthropology in respect of women.[3] It seems clear from Sayers's own memoirs, however, that from her parents she received unequivocal encouragement for her education; for with university entrance in mind, she needed competitive preparation for it, and this required attendance at boarding school. Her parents chose the Godolphin School, Salisbury, to which she was sent at age 15.

Contrary to her experience in her father's parish, the experience of Divinity at the Godolphin School was devoid of clear thinking and robbed of all drama in its presentation. She found herself confronted with dull lessons on biblical texts and with 'unctuous and unintellectual' reference to matters important for confirmation. Her parents preferred her to be confirmed while at school; but, looking back on this dimension of her life, she could not be other than fiercely critical of what had been on offer there. Doctrine was divorced from the business of living and, in any case, was not made a subject for clear thinking. Cathedrals and churches were both architecturally and visually devoid of colour, just as Divinity seemed to be devoid of the drama of dogma.[4] Fortunately, in the intervening years between school and the writing of her memoirs, she must have had many opportunities to visit newly built churches exemplifying the Gothic revival, which was more to her intellectual and High Church taste and provided visual sustenance for her own attempts to convey her passionately intelligent response to Christian belief.

Sayers's experience in a clergyman's household enabled her to write perceptively about the clergy and the role they might play in others' lives. One thinks of the rector, Mr Venables, in *The Nine Tailors* (1934), in tandem with Mrs Venables and her talent for organization; or of the Reverend Simon Goodacre in *Busman's Honeymoon* (1937), whose wife, with Mrs Venables, is the epitome of hospitality. In Sayers's writing there are no such damning caricatures of the clergy as may be found in the work of C. S. Lewis!

Defective though she had found Divinity at school, those who taught her other subjects prepared her effectively for entry to Somerville College, Oxford in 1912. University graduates at that time composed about two per cent of the population in the United Kingdom, so that university entrance placed Sayers among a very favoured few, and she worked hard to merit it.

Sayers was well through her courses of study by the time the First World War broke out, but she was far from untouched by it, as her early published poetry reveals. Her 'Hymn in Contemplation of Sudden Death' was written during the First World War, though it came again into its own during the aerial bombing of civilians in the Second. Sayers's detective fiction also shows the influence of the war upon her, as she reflects there the world of those men traumatized by the first 'European War', taking comfort, when they could afford it, in their clubs, where they found companionship with others also recovering from their experiences.

Anyone pioneering a professional life such as Sayers's had to interact with those who had survived physical wounds on the battlefield and often carried within them deep but hidden emotional scars from their experiences, as did C. S. Lewis and J. R. R. Tolkien. The universities were full of both teachers and taught who had shared terrible experiences; and, like towns and villages all over Britain, Oxford and Cambridge colleges held constant reminders of the war in the memorials placed within them – with the lists of names to be extended after 1945.

Sayers's response to the political situation between the wars included her awareness that all are complicit in the sinfulness that causes conflict. In the Second World War she found ways both of reflecting on war and also of enabling others to do so. But at the tail end of the Great War, her first responsibility to herself was to find a way of earning her living while also negotiating a series of possible love-relationships, for the war had made problematic the availability for marriage of men of her social class and education. A man who was not 'marriageable' became the father of her only son, Anthony, whom she had to find work to support. Initially she arranged for the child to be brought up by a trusted friend. Then, when she did find an appropriately marriageable man, she and her husband legally adopted him.

In a register office in 1926, Sayers married 'Mac', a divorced veteran whose children from his first marriage did not live with him. This marriage, too, became something of a problem, as Mac was unable to make his way in the world as successfully as he had hoped. Yet by comparison with the abysmal circumstances of other discharged soldiers, and considering the atrocious housing, education and medical services available to them, Sayers and her husband did not do too badly between them.

Between the wars, Sayers became a public figure with a distinct-ively courageous Christian voice, for in her detective fiction she had already explored in imagined flesh and blood the possibility and difficulty of living such Christian principles as the commitments to truth and justice. Because of economic depression, the rise of fascist and totalitarian governments in Europe and another and more terrible war to endure, little changed for the majority of the population until after 1945. But change was gravely needed, and because of the voice she had established, Sayers was asked to contribute to the thinking ahead which needed to be undertaken. In each genre she worked in – whether detective stories, political essays or plays – she made Christian understanding central. By the late 1930s, she had begun to get dogma on stage.

Detective fiction and theological reflection

Sayers's first publishing success – apart, that is, from her writing of advertising slogans and copy for the firm that employed her – was *Whose Body?* (1923). Over the years, her detective, Peter Wimsey, impossible fantasy-figure though he is, endeared himself to detective-fiction readers as she developed his portrait, using him to explore a variety of personal, moral, social and even religious issues. Wimsey is an aristocrat, from a family still able to maintain the estates which he might inherit if his nephew manages to kill himself driving a car at speed – a trait the nephew shares with his uncle. He has been educated at public school, singing in his local parish church choir during the holidays at his ducal home and no doubt attending Balliol College chapel while at Oxford. He is a useful bell-ringer, and under-stands the decent arrangement of churches, not least the great churches of the Fens. He is somewhat reticent about religion, but is well acquainted with biblical texts, especially with the Psalms, and reads lessons well if asked to do so. He is an accomplished cricketer as well as pianist, with a special affection for Bach; he collects first editions; he writes elegant and scholarly monographs when the fancy takes him; he manages his money with great success; he gets on well with an astonishing range of people; he has a good range of languages to his credit, much valued by the Foreign Office when on occasion he is recruited as a free-range diplomat. Sayers focuses on Wimsey's miseries until another survivor of the trenches, a non-commissioned soldier, turns up to care for him in the then familiar role of 'gentleman's gentleman'. Bunter and he become inseparable, not least because Bunter can cope with Wimsey's shell-shock and his memory of having had to give orders that sent so many to their deaths.

And Peter Wimsey can and does take his pick from time to time of the beautiful and accomplished women who become his mistresses. Harriet Vane, whom he eventually marries, is a woman of intelligence, though no great beauty, whom he first encounters when she is on trial for the murder of her lover. Crucial to establishing her innocence, he then has to wait for over five years until in and through her own work – the writing of detective fiction – she comes to understand that he does indeed fully appreciate her need to sort herself out after this episode in her life, and that she has remained true to her abilities as a writer. At that point, they are able to marry, and Harriet gains not only a mother-in-law who takes her to her own heart but also the admirable Bunter. Companion-sleuth to Peter, Bunter accompanies him in his Daimler wherever he goes, seeing to it that an ample supply of wine is carefully cradled in an eiderdown in the back of the vehicle when Peter and Harriet set off on their honeymoon – with Bunter also in the back.

Peter loathes violence and destruction, and much of the point of his diplomatic endeavours is to stave off further chaos in Europe. At home, however, his determination to resist chaos takes the form of detection, including murder cases, which especially have their cost for him. In one instance, he rings in the New Year, only to discover some time later that, along with the other bell-ringers, he has killed a wrongdoer tied up above the bell-ringing platform in the bell-tower. On this occasion, he has to accept the judgment of the rector, Mr Venables: 'Perhaps God speaks through those mouths of inarticulate metal. He is a righteous judge, strong and patient, and is provoked every day.'[5] Here Sayers seems to wonder whether humans can ever be truly just. Is it possible that even in our efforts to be just we do injustice? Or is it that God manages to accomplish justice even though our efforts so frequently fail?

Revisiting her former Oxford college sometime after being completely cleared of the accusation of murder, Harriet recognizes in the members of the Senior Common Room their shared integrity in the pursuit of truth, come what may. Peter himself writes to her that he knows that 'if you have put anything in hand, disagreeableness and danger will not turn you back, and God forbid they should'. The principled pursuit of truth has meant the ruin of one man's career by one of the dons, and Harriet is instrumental in uncovering the fact and its consequences in the disruptions it brings to the college. Peter can only say that he admits the principle that the consequences must follow, and refers to the biblical words about bringing not peace but a sword.[6]

On their honeymoon, however, Harriet quails when Peter finds himself with evidence that they simply must put to the police, despite the fact that they now know the persons who may be involved in the death which concerns them. True to his principles, Peter simply says, 'It's evidence. We can't pick and choose. Whoever suffers, we *must* have the truth. Nothing else matters a damn.' And Harriet agrees with him: 'The thing has got to be done. By any means, so long as we get to the bottom of it. That's your job, and it's worth doing.' The problem is that in this case the job involves the death sentence for the murderer, and both Bunter and Harriet have to see Peter through the night before the execution by hanging. As Peter says, 'If there *is* a God or a judgment – what next? What have we done?'[7]

Thinking toward social renewal

Through – and, one might even say, despite – the extraordinary character of Peter, Sayers was profoundly serious about the issues involved; that is, about how justice and truth were to live and flourish among not merely human frailty but downright wickedness. When the difficulties of the 1920s and 1930s finally led to the Second World War, Sayers was among those asked to think ahead about the direction society should take. Becoming even more serious about the issues, Sayers observed, in a 1942 address, that 'war is a judgment that overtakes societies when they have been living upon ideas that conflict too violently with the laws governing the universe'.[8]

The only way forward is to think truly about the nature of God, of humankind, indeed of reality as a whole. That true understanding, she believed, was to be found in Christian dogma; and Christian dogma is, when all is said and done, truth known through images. The central dogma of the Incarnation, for example, directly affirms that Christ is in his human concreteness the perfect 'image of the Image of the Unimaginable'.[9] Because the perfect image is the eternal

Son of God made incarnate in a particular time and place, the image can only be known in the poetic imagery of story and event, never as abstract philosophical principle. Therefore, Sayers believed, her contribution required that she take us to 'the place of the images'.[10]

As Sayers and others came most painfully to realize, issues of truth and justice were at the heart of the troubles leading up to the First World War and to the growing difficulties following it. It was far from easy to understand how to proceed. Ireland and its relationship to Parliament in London was a long-standing and apparently irresolvable matter, quite apart from the social, emotional and political legacy of the war and the problems precipitated by the conditions of 'peace' at its end. Few with direct experience or reliable information about the First World War's battlefields, graveyards, commemorations and survivors would be likely to view the possibility of yet another major conflict with other than the gravest misgivings. It was in this war, and not just in industrialized cities, that men had become 'matter' at the mercy of 'machines'. Few were clear about the need to prepare against any future possible disaster by reconstructing their armed forces, or had the energy to rethink how conflict might be conducted if war broke out again.

The most thoughtful – including Sayers – were alert to the legacies of imperialism, certainly the source of some benefits but also of accompanying conflict and brutality, which would surely at some point involve wars of liberation from occupying power. And there was information enough about the results of the Russian Revolution of 1917 to make 'communism' the prime bogey: the centralization of the USSR, the havoc wrought upon its peoples by collectivization, the establishment of labour camps and settlements, the shifting of whole populations, the multiplicity of deaths and then the show trials of 1936–38.

But the evidence of a comparable menace much closer to home in the rise of the Third Reich was missed by many. Shamefully, the capitulation of Germany's universities, the 'German Church' movement, the exodus of immense talent of all kinds from Germany in the wake of the collapse of the Weimar Republic and the rise of National Socialism were not widely recognized for what they were. And, as part of their reluctance to precipitate another international war, European governments failed to support the Republicans in the Spanish Civil War. Spain exemplified not only the horrors of civil war but also the alleged defence of 'Christendom' by the forces of General Franco. Furthermore, the papacy, having lost its estates at the end of the nineteenth century, was preoccupied with securing the institution of the Roman Catholic Church by the negotiation of concordats, as, for example, with fascist Mussolini in Italy. In view of these events, it seemed far from irresponsible to think that putting right some of the wrongs inflicted on Germany by the Versailles Treaty of 1919 would make an all-out war less rather than more likely.

Unfortunately, by seriously underestimating the ambitions of the new German Chancellor, other European governments missed the opportunity to block those ambitions. By the time they were confronted with the realities of occupation by a Nazi regime, it was too late. Czechoslovakia was abandoned to Germany by the very governments that had created it; and the Yugoslav army, influenced by vivid memories of the origins of the First World War, offered virtually no resistance to German invasion. The Balkans were carved up into German and Italian 'spheres of influence', and, like the Vichy government in France, the German and Italian occupiers implemented Nazi policies toward 'opponents' with camps eventually set up for mass killings on Polish soil. The fate of Poland pushed the United Kingdom into the war.

In a way, the war and its austerities were comparable to those of Sayers's childhood and youth, since so much of what seemed to matter to her contemporaries was of no lasting concern to her personally, and she was undoubtedly capable of a certain asceticism when it was called for, as her strictures on such deadly sins as gluttony and covetousness also reveal. No sooner had the war got under way, however, than she was among those who responded to the invitation to contribute to the much-needed rethinking about the future of her society. This was to take her well out of her earlier range of work, but by this time her overall position was well worked out and needed but restating in the confidence that the allies would be victorious in the longer run.

As she began thinking toward British renewal, Sayers insisted that it was high time the doctrines of God as creator and of humankind as God's image be fully assimilated and consistently acted upon. We must, she believed, attend to the possible connection between ignoring the Christian truth about human beings and the increasing frequency and extent of wars. Because the first truth about God is that God is creator, the essential nature of human beings is that they, too, are creators. From this recognition flow all manner of truths about what persons are for, what work is and how persons are to live in relation to God and in human society. As creative agents, people must look forward, not back; they must overcome habitual inertia; they must acquire such knowledge as they can, make it part of their experience and act on it for themselves. They must exercise creative imagination in thinking out what kind of society is wanted based on the recognition that as images of God all human persons are equal in the sight of God, responsible to God and with rights to freedom and fulfilment.

Continuing the work of thinking out the ramifications of Christian belief for the British future, Sayers claimed that all who understood the Athanasian Creed well knew that nothing in matter, time and space had absolute value. That was true only of God, uncreated, incomprehensible and eternal, and could not be true even of desperately desired peace. Given German cruelty and opportunism, and despite the incompetence, shortcomings and sins that she saw in herself and in her compatriots, Sayers believed that the war against Germany was 'just'. Making her conviction even stronger was the utter opposition of the Christian understanding of God and humankind to the hideous ethical meaning of Nazism, which she describes with great passion in a 1940 address.[11] Thus the war with Germany had to be endured.

But it was crucial to have learned from the end of the First World War, when, in direct contravention of Christian principles, peace had been dictated rather than negotiated, the principles advocated by the United States had not been honoured, and reparations and humiliations had been heaped on the defeated enemy.[12] Furthermore, there was no need to await disaster from the air to get on with the business of dealing with the carelessness and incompetence which had produced ill-housed, ill-fed, ill-clothed, ill-behaved and verminous children who had to be evacuated from cities to avoid the bombing.[13] Above all, infinite patience and sympathy would be required after the war in dealing with the German people 'if we are to make them understand our intentions at all, and we shall have to be very sure that those intentions are, in fact, unselfish and liberal, as well as just and firm, and that they are undertaken in a really constructive spirit'.[14]

Unfortunately, such intentions were hardly expressed in some aspects of British policy as it developed during the war.

Looking back, we can see that, in addition to her wartime addresses and essays, Sayers's contributions to British renewal involved three major projects of the imagination: the writing and production of plays, the aesthetic and theological essay *The Mind of the Maker* and the translation of Dante's *Divine Comedy*. Distinct as these projects may seem, they are related, and imagination is at their heart.

Even before the Second World War began and before there was an explicit invitation to British intellectuals to rethink British life, Sayers had begun to write plays, and play-writing became very much an intentional part of her renewal contribution. In 1938, in an article invited by the *Sunday Times* for Passion Sunday, Sayers put forth the claim that became the platform on which the rest of her work would stand: 'The Christian faith is the most exciting drama that ever staggered the imagination of man – and the dogma *is* the drama.'[15] She began to make a case for this claim by doing what no one else had the temerity to do: put on stage the substance of orthodox Christian belief in its creedal form and patristic exposition.

For those within reach of Canterbury Cathedral, whose governing body had boldly commissioned a series of plays to be performed therein (including T. S. Eliot's *Murder in the Cathedral* and Charles Williams's *Thomas Cranmer of Canterbury*), Sayers wrote *The Zeal of Thy House* for 1937. In it she made the integrity of one's work the central theme, though the play also looks ahead to her treatment of the Trinity in *The Mind of the Maker*. On Christmas Day 1938 her Nativity play, *He That Should Come*, was broadcast. Then came the quite singular achievement of the cycle of 12 radio plays, *The Man Born to be King*, the first of which was broadcast on 21 December 1941. More cathedral plays followed: *The Just Vengeance*, for the Lichfield Festival in 1946, and *The Emperor Constantine*, for the Colchester Festival in 1951. All these works take us to 'the place of the images' where the drama of Christian dogma is presented.

While she was writing plays, Sayers produced her most important and influential theological essay, *The Mind of the Maker*. Although it is neither a novel nor a play but an essay in aesthetics and theology, it is very much a part of the project to make clear the drama of Christian faith, to appropriate its wisdom in thinking beyond the war to the renewal of British life and, especially, to show us the images.

This essay explores the biblical idea that human beings are images of God, and it does so in a way that helps make sense both of God as trinity of persons and of human beings as creative agents. Sayers believed that the reappropriation of this understanding of what we essentially are can help toward a more just economic and social life. What we know first and best about God is that God is creator, and what we know first and best about ourselves is that we are created in the image of God. But if we are images of God, then we, too, are creators. And if our dignity as images of God is to be respected, then social, political and economic life must be so ordered that persons can express their creativity and so fulfil their human nature.

Drawing on her experience as a creative writer, Sayers develops this analogy. Human persons have the capacity to form an 'idea' of something to be accomplished or brought to concreteness – as a writer has an idea for a book that can be written. In this ability, persons are like God the Father creator, except that in God the vision of the whole to be created is complete, perfect and truly timeless. Again, the human artist sets about expressing or giving concrete body to the vision. In this activity of expressing the vision, persons are like the incarnation of the eternal Son – except, again, that the human expression will not be a perfect enactment of the creator's vision, as is the incarnate Christ. Finally, the creative artist will imbue the embodiment of the vision with meaning that will be effectively felt by and communicated to others. In this power to communicate and enliven, the artist's work is like the Holy Spirit.

Here, then, are three elements in dynamic relation with each other: Vision-Activity-Power. They can be distinguished, but they cannot in reality be separated. Each is, in its way, the whole work. Thus, human creative activity teaches us the essentially trinitarian nature of God. Sayers's analogy validates the creative aspect of ourselves; in it we see that in our creative capacity and activity we are like God. In the light of this image we can evaluate not only our own work and lives but also social policy and structure.

In these terms, Sayers insisted on the importance of attention to political and economic life and laid the foundations for a Christian aesthetic of many different kinds of work. She firmly repudiated any nonsense about religious faith being the merely 'private' affair of an individual. If it is of importance anywhere, then the gift of creative imagination is surely of crucial significance for the life of the 'city', for the life for which we are all mutually responsible, as her reappropriation of Dante was to demonstrate. Thus, Sayers had a most generous view of what it means to believe in Christ as the incarnation of the eternal Son of God.[16] Her view made her sharply and justly critical of the kinds of work it was proper to undertake if a sense of 'vocation in work' was to be advanced in the world after the Second World War.[17]

The third of Sayers's efforts toward British renewal is her translation of Dante's *Divine Comedy*. It might seem that translating a piece of medieval literature is a long way from getting the dogma on stage and thinking toward the British future. It is not. In fact, the project is a practice of what she preached in *The Mind of the Maker* and as much a matter of showing us the images as is the writing of plays. *The Divine Comedy* and *The Just Vengeance* are intimately related and mutually clarifying.

Sayers had first-hand experience of spending nights in air-raid shelters, and it was during such nights that, as a result of reading Charles Williams's *The Figure of Beatrice* (1943), she plunged into the rereading of the whole of Dante's *Divine Comedy* in the original. Just as Dante had related his vision to the circumstances of his day, so Sayers related Dante to hers; and it was no wonder that his great work of theological imagination and her reinterpretation of it spoke powerfully to readers immediately after the Second World War. But it was a new and terrifying dimension of warfare that made Dante's poetic theological vision especially powerful to Sayers and led her to write *The Just Vengeance*, in which she truly puts the dogmas of sin, Incarnation, Atonement and redemption on stage.

This new dimension of warfare, implemented by the US Army Air Force and the Royal Air Force with targets agreed with the Soviet Union, was the systematic destruction of German cities one after another in order to bring the war to an end, no matter the cost to their civilian populations. The saturation bombing of Cologne, Hamburg, Berlin and Dresden followed in February 1945, killing some 20,000 people. Apart from the tons of explosives, the bombers had become expert in creating 'fire-storms', which sucked oxygen out of the air. The victims in Dresden seem to have been largely those not directly employed in Germany's war effort: the old, women, children and thousands of refugees moving west. Whatever the details, the debate about whether the bombing is to be categorized as a war crime continues. There is no question, however, that Sayers saw sinfulness on all sides. She had pondered intentional and unintentional guilt in her detective novels. She now returned to explore the universality of guilt in relation to the means of atonement through the Incarnation, crucifixion and resurrection: the drama of human life in the light of the drama of Christian doctrine.

Sayers became aware of the impossibility of escaping injustice even in a war that must be fought for the sake of justice. Her memoirs reveal that at school she had had a much-respected teacher of music, Fräulein Fehmer, who had returned to Frankfurt and become an ardent Nazi. Sayers's poem 'Target Area' (1944) imagines her old teacher under the onslaught of the bombers. Imagination gave her eyes to see what mere awareness of facts could not – that there is a sense in which she herself, in willing the end of the war, has willed the means: filling the bombs, loading the bomb-racks, building the planes, equipping the young men who fly them.[18] She knows that 'all men stand convicted of blood / in the High Court, the judge with the accused', that our solidarity is in guilt and that even our virtues need forgiveness.[19] She now had to confront on the mass scale of war the very issues she had to some extent explored in her detective fiction in respect of the murder of individuals.

Dante's *Divine Comedy* became her theological source. In Canto XXI of *Purgatory* she found the phrase that became the title of *The Just Vengeance*, the cathedral play which she deemed to be her best, written for Lichfield Cathedral's 750th anniversary in 1946. Of considerable importance, however, was her attention to the fact that the exposition of the phrase 'the just vengeance' does not come in Dante until Canto VI of *Paradise*:

> Herein the Living Justice maketh sweet
> All our affections, which can never be
> Perverted now to vice or lusts unmeet.[20]

Beatrice, Dante's personal and most beloved mediator of grace, then explains the just vengeance in Canto VII. Its meaning had been familiar from Anselm's *Why God Became Man*, to the effect that man owes God his praise, yet in his dispraise of God he has made himself incapable of that praise, and cannot put himself back into right relationship with God. In Dante the conclusion of the argument in Canto VII reads:

> For God's self-giving, which made possible
> That man should raise himself, showed more largesse
> Than if by naked power He'd cancelled all;
> And every other means would have been less
> Than justice, if it had not *pleased* God's Son
> To be humiliate into fleshliness.[21]

The crucial point here is that the doctrines of Atonement and redemption are appropriately understood only with the recognition that they involve on God's part the experience of the grace, joy and delight of salvation. But how to put this point across to an audience? Here is a high challenge for the imagination, and it is the power of Sayers's play to present the crucifixion of the God-Man not as an act of a bloodthirsty God with a lust for vindictive justice but as a gracious, joyous and beautiful act of self-giving by God on our behalf.

Sayers takes a bold step in setting the action in an instant of time as an airman is shot down during the war from his bomber. So downed, he finds himself in the whole company of those who have inhabited Lichfield and among whom he experiences the drama of the Incarnation, crucifixion and resurrection. Eventually he chooses Christ crucified, though he begins by being overwhelmed with agony about his role in the recent conflict, in which there seemed to have been 'no choice except between bloody alternatives'.[22] The remedy is presented as the Choir pleads to Mary to choose 'the weight of glory', invoking the first six lines of Canto XXXIII of *Paradise*, the hymn to the Virgin, 21 lines of which Dorothy was to translate and send to her friends as a Christmas greeting in 1949 and which were then incorporated by Barbara Reynolds as she completed the translation of *Paradise*. The lines sung by the Choir include these words:

> Thou are that she by whom our human nature
> Was so ennobled that it might become
> The Creator to create himself the creature.

In Sayers's play it is Eve who dreads the vengeance of God after Abel's murder by her other son, Cain, and who pleads for

> A kind of mercy that is not unjust,
> A not unmerciful justice – if we could see it;
> Something that, once seen, would commend itself,
> Not to be argued with.[23]

Sayers wants her argument put in bodily form, presented not as an abstraction but as an image, concretely. As in reality God has given us in the Incarnation the perfection of the image of God, the image we were created to be but which we have despoiled, so in the play the perfect image comes as the 'Persona Dei' (the Son, the second person of the Trinity), divesting himself of crown and majesty, offering himself as bread and wine to the airman, a body broken

> That I, in you, may break and give yourselves
> For all the world. No man has greater love
> Than he who lays his life down for his friends.[24]

The airman lets himself go 'into Thy hand, O God', and the Persona Dei praises those who bear with him

> the bitter burden of things
> In patience, or, being burdened without choice,
> Choose only to be patient

and who finally choose him who has himself set his feet in Hell.[25]

The last, splendid piece for the Choir invites the 'good and faithful servants' to enter into the joy of their Lord, to praise God with 'the glorious and holy flesh', with 'the moving and sensitive heart' and with 'the searching and subtle brain',[26] which is Sayers's response to Canto XIV of *Paradise*. It is to Solomon that Dante gives praise of 'the holy and glorious flesh', not simply because he was believed to have written the Song of Songs, but also because he embodied royal and divinely given wisdom. So to him can be given the privilege of expounding the doctrine of the resurrection of the body, to which Sayers in her turn attempted to do justice. Inspired by Dante, she became a poet of the divine generosity.

In the decade or so left to her, Sayers's main achievement was to translate Dante's *Divine Comedy*, to comment on it in such a way as to render it intelligible not only to scholars of Italian literature but also to those who needed to understand Christian doctrine and its profound significance for their lives in the aftermath of a terrible war. As she had seen, justice and truth could not be perceived without intellectual integrity in all aspects of life, not least in economic and political life; nor could they be seen without the standard contained in essential Christian doctrines, themselves known in images that present them in the drama of their concreteness.

In our new age of airborne terror, of plastic landmines and home-made explosives, we need Sayers's willingness to address what is happening and to find resources to help us relate to God in and through it all. We cannot hope to approach her level of achievement, but we can at least aspire to see with her that we are images of God and that the content of faith is dramatic and liveable belief.

Notes

1 Dorothy L. Sayers, *The Just Vengeance* (London: Victor Gollancz, 1946), p. 47.

2 Sayers, *Just Vengeance*, p. 47.

3 Dorothy L. Sayers, 'Are Women Human?' and 'The Human-Not-Quite-Human', in *Unpopular Opinions* (London: Victor Gollancz, 1946), pp. 106–16, 116–22.

4 Dorothy L. Sayers, *Child and Woman of Her Time*, vol. 5 of *The Letters of Dorothy L. Sayers*, ed. Barbara Reynolds (Cambridge: Dorothy L. Sayers Society, 2002), pp. 107–15, 135.

5 Dorothy L. Sayers, *The Nine Tailors* (1934; repr., London: New English Library, 1982), p. 298.

6 Dorothy L. Sayers, *Gaudy Night* (1935; repr., London: New English Library, 1970), pp. 208, 430.

7 Dorothy L. Sayers, *Busman's Honeymoon* (1937; repr., London: New English Library, 1977), pp. 301, 303, 395.

8 Dorothy L. Sayers, 'Why Work?' (1942), in *Creed or Chaos?* (New York: Harcourt, Brace, 1949), p. 47.

9 Sayers, *Just Vengeance*, p. 52.

10 Sayers, *Just Vengeance*, p. 47.

11 Sayers, 'Why Work?', pp. 25–30.

12 Dorothy L. Sayers, *Begin Here: A Statement of Faith* (New York: Harcourt, Brace, 1941), pp. 139–44.

13 Sayers, *Begin Here*, pp. 151–2.

14 Sayers, *Begin Here*, p. 147.

15 Dorothy L. Sayers, *The Greatest Drama Ever Staged* (London: Hodder and Stoughton, 1938), p. 6.

16 Dorothy L. Sayers, *The Mind of the Maker* (1941; repr., San Francisco: HarperSanFrancisco, 1987), chs 2, 3 and 6; and 'What Do We Believe?', in *Unpopular Opinions*, pp. 17–20.

17 Sayers, 'Why Work?', pp. 46–62.

18 Dorothy L. Sayers, *The Poetry of Dorothy L. Sayers*, ed. Ralph E. Hone (Cambridge: Dorothy L. Sayers Society in association with the Marion E. Wade Center, 1996), pp. 140–4.

19 Sayers, *Poetry*, p. 144.
20 Dante Alighieri, *Paradise*, trans. Dorothy L. Sayers and Barbara Reynolds (Harmondsworth: Penguin, 1962), VI, 121–3.
21 Dante, *Paradise* VII, 115–20. Emphasis added.
22 Sayers, *Just Vengeance*, p. 18.
23 Sayers, *Just Vengeance*, p. 45.
24 Sayers, *Just Vengeance*, p. 58.
25 Sayers, *Just Vengeance*, pp. 76, 78.
26 Sayers, *Just Vengeance*, pp. 79, 80.

Figure 4 Charles Williams.
Used by permission of The Marion E. Wade Center,
Wheaton College, Wheaton, IL.

4

Charles Williams: Words, images and (the) Incarnation

CHARLES HEFLING

Because in Him the Flesh is united to the Word without magical transformation, Imagination is redeemed from promiscuous fornication with her own images.

W. H. Auden

Now that Lewis and Tolkien have won the distinction of having their fiction made into motion pictures, will another Inkling be next? The 'frank supernaturalism and the frankly bloodcurdling episodes'[1] that Lewis himself found remarkable in the seven novels of Charles Williams would seem to be just the sort of thing that computer-generated imaging was made for. There is a pterodactyl, for instance, and a sorcerer who makes a pseudo-body out of dust and spittle for two disembodied souls. It is true that Williams did not create an alternative universe, like Narnia or Middle-earth, and his stories offer little in the way of exotic spectacle. They are set in utterly ordinary places and peopled, for the most part, with utterly ordinary characters. But that only enhances the eeriness of the utterly extraordinary situations and states of being into which these characters are drawn. A pterodactyl is much the sort of thing anyone might see in Middle-earth. The one in *The Place of the Lion* appears at the window of a pedantic student poring over a dry-as-dust research thesis, and the effect would be all the more uncanny if it could be not only visualized but, literally, seen.

Or so it seems. On the other hand, there can be some doubt as to whether a Williams novel, 'translated' off the page and on to the screen, would still be a Williams novel. Any adaptation of written fiction for cinematic purposes has to sacrifice something, but in the case of Williams's fiction the sacrifice would be Williams. Almost by definition, his writing *as* writing would not survive the transformation. The plot and the dialogue might be scrupulously preserved, but the *style* would disappear – and style, for Williams, was no optional extra. To quote a maxim he fully endorsed, style is oneself; *le style, c'est l'homme même.* T. S. Eliot, who knew him personally, wrote that never had he known a writer 'who was more wholly the same man in his life and in his writings'.[2] Reading Williams's novels, the later ones especially, is not only entering a fictional world: it is meeting an author, and an author who was, after all – or rather, before all – a poet. His poems are few, in comparison with the 40 books of prose he wrote, but he did not cease to be the poet, the 'maker', the verbal craftsman, when he turned from verse to literary criticism or history or theology. If, he declared, 'one is anxious to write about God, one ought to be anxious to write well'.[3] If one is anxious to write, say, detective fiction, the prescription is the same. None of Williams's own novels fits that description (though *War in Heaven* begins as if it might), but he reviewed a great many whodunits, and Jared Lobdell, having tracked down these reviews, rightly calls attention to how often Williams distributes praise or blame on account of style.[4]

Colourful, dramatic, imaginative – Williams's novels are all that, but before all that they are literature. The words, and the way he uses them, are essential. The decidedly individual Williams style is not one that appeals to everyone's taste, and when it does the taste is usually acquired. Sixty years ago, Eliot could commend the novels as 'first of all very good reading, say on a train journey or an air flight', but there was a hint of special pleading even then. They can, certainly, be read for entertainment, and Eliot is right in saying that Williams would have liked them to be so read – the first time. But it is also true that they resist being read with half the reader's mind on something else. While the writing is by no means as difficult as it is in Williams's poems, for which Lewis felt the need to write a lavish commentary, it does require some effort.

There is the diction, to begin with – compact, epigrammatic, a little mannered, sometimes eccentric, always polished. And there are the allusions. Not every sentence in a Williams novel includes verbal echoes of Augustine, Horace, Dante and St Paul, but one sentence in *Descent into Hell* does, and it is not altogether untypical. Williams is not displaying erudition for the sake of display; the sentence does advance his narrative and say something about one of his characters.

Also, however, it says something about the novel itself and about the novelist. No great damage is done to the story, as story, if Augustine's words go unrecognized. But what the story is a story *about* was for Williams a fact, a reality, on which estimable persons, Augustine and the rest, have had something worthwhile to say. Alluding to what they said is a matter of personal as well as literary style – a courteous nod to greater colleagues. At the same time, it serves to position Williams's own presentation of the relevant fact within a cultural tradition. However insignificant the people in his novels may be in themselves, they are subject to experiences that have been held to be the most significant experiences anyone can have. Sometimes they grasp the significance, sometimes not, but Williams hopes the reader will grasp it, not least by means of his literary signals. In the same novel, what he says about the words and deeds of a certain minor figure gives attentive readers all they need to know in order to assess her motives and her character. But he also gives her a name: Lily Sammile. Who Lilith and Samael were – or are – is not indispensable information, but it does suggest that hers is a perennial role.

Such devices are not unique to Williams, of course. They may be effective. They may not. They are, in any case, *literary* devices of a kind that is not easily transferred into another medium. Nor are they separable from Williams's use of imagery as such. Certainly not all the images in his novels draw, as the embedded quotations do, on a canon of great literature. There is nothing very bookish about a pterodactyl, and often enough the imagery is 'archetypal' in the sense of being universally recognizable, if not in the quasi-Jungian sense of being built into every human consciousness. *The Place of the Lion* is the most extended example. More complex, and more interesting in this regard, is *The Greater Trumps*, which can be read as a novel about imagination itself – its power, its dangers and its ambiguity. The novel's 'archetypal' images are drawn from the Tarot, a deck of 78 cards used in divination. The four suits into which the minor cards are divided correspond to the primal elements – earth, air, fire, water – out of which all things are constituted. This quaternity figures prominently throughout the novel, but even more prominent are the 22 cards known as 'major arcana' or 'greater trumps', each of which depicts a prescribed scene or figure. As one of the characters puts it (or tries), the trumps 'are the truths – the facts – call them what you will – principles of thought, actualities of corporate existence, Death and Love and certain Virtues and Meditation and the Benign Sun of Wisdom, and so on. You must see them – there aren't any words to tell you.'[5]

Here then is a panoply of symbolic images that are meaningful yet obscure, open to any number of interpretations while stipulating none. This semiotic indeterminacy is no doubt what led Williams to build a novel around the Tarot. It is also a theme of the novel he built. Nobody (in the story) knows where the cards came from; none of them has a fixed meaning; no text or authority or tradition settles what their symbols stand for. The significance of the trumps is as polyvalent as the primal elements. The Tarot thus represents and releases a kind of unformed, unregulated, unspecific imaginative energy that has, in itself, no moral or intellectual finality. In Williams's novel it interacts with another symbolic universe that is just the opposite – formal, regulated, specific. Chaotic indeterminacy encounters creative order. To put it a little less abstractly, what happens in the story is that violent, elemental forces, set loose through a supernatural set of Tarot cards, are brought under control and subsumed within a peaceable pattern that has its verbal diagram in the precise and unambiguous formulation of Christian dogma known as the Creed of St Athanasius. Williams arranges his plot so that the denouement takes place shortly after this definition of faith (which he once called a 'great humanist Ode'[6]) has been sung in a village church, on one of the days of the year for which the Book of Common Prayer appoints it. The day is Christmas. *The Greater Trumps* is among other things a Christmas story, in which exotic Magi, the magical trumps, do homage to the incarnate Word, as defined in the most exact of the Christian creeds.

All this may sound as though the novel is a fantasia on theologico-philosophical hermeneutics. It is nothing of the sort. William Lindsay Gresham's exuberant description stands: *The Greater Trumps* is 'a slam-bang action-fantasy melodrama'.[7] What is, however, true is that like the other novels – like everything Williams wrote – it is the work of a mind possessed by what can only be called a vivid apprehension of the wholeness of things. It is a Christian apprehension, certainly. But for Williams 'Christianity and life ought to be one; no doubt, essentially, they *are* one.'[8] The Athanasian Creed is a humanist ode precisely because 'the great doctrines are only the statement of something as wide as the universe and as deep as the human heart. . . . The

Christian Church has been charged with the great secrets which are the only facts of existence.[9] Not that *Trumps*, or any of the other novels, is clandestine apologetics, a doctrinal treatise decked out in narrative. Williams was quite capable of expounding and commending Christian dogma, but he did it in writings that wear their purpose on their faces. There will be more to say about those writings. In the novels he is doing something else. There, to quote Eliot again, 'Williams is telling us about a world of experience known to him: he does not merely persuade us to believe in something, he communicates this experience.'[10] One might wish to quarrel with 'experience', a word that raises as many questions as it answers. 'World' is equally important. Williams might have said that he was trying to communicate an order, a pattern, a constellation of which only a part is or ever can be grasped in any single moment of experience. The whole of it is all-inclusive. Someone with a philosophical turn of mind might have called this totality Being. Williams called it the glory of God.

'Glory', he observes, usually means something like a mazy, bright blur. 'But the maze should be, though it generally is not, exact, and the brightness should be that of a geometrical pattern.'[11] Heaven, like the Athanasian Creed, is precise and orderly. Hell is always inaccurate. Between the one and the other, for the time being, 'The glory of God is in facts. The almost incredible nature of things is that there is no fact which is not in His glory.'[12] Any experience that discloses and makes credible this almost incredible nature of things is itself one of the facts comprised in what Williams is wont to call 'the pattern of the glory'. If slam-bang action-fantasy melodrama communicates the experience, or even the possibility of such an experience, it does what its author intended.

In this regard, as in others, Williams's master was Dante. About Dante and *The Divine Comedy* he wrote a great deal, including the book that is often regarded as the best of his non-fiction, *The Figure of Beatrice*. To compare his own fiction with Dante's great poem is perhaps presumptuous, but not so presumptuous as it might seem. *The Divine Comedy* is, among other things, an imagined narrative, allusively and elaborately symbolic, with a formal structure that is mathematically orderly, and not without its slam-bang, melodramatic episodes. Williams admired it unstintingly on all counts. But the more pertinent points of comparison are two. First, the events that Dante narrates are at once sequential stages in an 'otherworld journey' and progressive stages in the transformation of a soul. The poem has an outward, 'literal' sense and an inward, 'anagogical' sense, as the poet himself explained. Second, both the writing of the *Comedy* and the progress it describes began with a certain event, a single incident, a fact – the same fact that pervades *The Greater Trumps*. Dante the poet found himself in the existential state of being called romantic love.

It is not an uncommon state. Dorothy L. Sayers, whom Williams inspired to translate the *Comedy*, tells of his sitting in a barber's chair, having his hair cut, and hearing the barber say that when his sweet-heart was with him he felt he had not an enemy in the world and could forgive anyone for anything. Whereupon Williams jumped from the chair to shout, 'My dear man, that's exactly what Dante said!'[13] What had happened in Florence was happening in London, 600 years of cultural change notwithstanding. 'The thing happens,' as Williams was fond of saying. Yet, momentous though it is for anyone to whom it does happen, the 'Beatrician moment' is less important than what happens next. To be content with what has happened already, as though it were complete in itself, is to prefer 'an immediately satisfy-ing experience of things to the believed pattern of the universe; one may even say, the pattern of the glory'.[14] Alternatively, the experience can be taken not as an end but as a beginning. 'There has been', Williams writes, 'and is, now as always, only one question about this state of things: is it serious? is it capable of intellectual treatment? is it capable of belief, labour, fruition? is it (in some sense or other) *true?*'[15] Dante took the second step: he asked those questions. *The Divine Comedy* is his answer.

Williams not only expounded Dante's answer but worked out his own, in the shape of the 'theology of romantic love' for which, next to his novels, he is best known. There is no need to analyse it in detail here. That has been done.[16] Briefly stated, its centre is the relation between two configurations; two archetypes, one might say. On the one hand is a particular aspect of the pattern of the glory, the aspect that Dante beheld in Beatrice (and the barber in his sweetheart); on the other, the clauses in the Athanasian Creed that define the Incarnation. Like life and Christianity, the two are coincident, or ought to be. In each there is unification, an at-one-ment, which occurs 'not by conversion of the Godhead into flesh', to quote Williams's favourite verse in the Creed, 'but by taking of the manhood into God'.

In the state of romantic love the humanity of the beloved *means* more than itself, and it means what it does in such a way as to include the lover in its meaning. Since that which is meant *is* love, *caritas*, it is accordingly required of the lover not only to be *in* but to *be* that love. The way that leads to meeting this requirement was the way that Dante began to follow from the time he first saw Beatrice. To follow that way, Williams allows, is entirely possible

> without introducing the name of God. But it is hardly possible to follow it without proposing and involving as an end a state of *caritas* of the utmost possible height and breadth, nor without allowing to matter a significance and power which (of all the religions and philoso-phies) only Christianity has affirmed.[17]

Inasmuch as romantic love has the same potentialities irrespective of the specific terms in which it is understood and communicated, Williams was open to a kind of 'anonymous Christianity'. That, it could be said, is what his novels are about.

The converse is equally true. Williams's non-fictional writings frequently apply the form and content of Christianity's foundational narrative directly to the psychic or affective or spiritual life of persons here and now. He found his warrant for the application in the narra-tive itself. The Gospel of John, on his reading, 'particularly stresses the fact that all the events in the life of our Lord, as well as happen-ing in Judæa, happen in the soul; whereas the Synoptics made it crashingly clear that all the events that happen in the soul happened in Judæa'.[18] Formally, this correspondence of inward and outward events parallels the twofold meaning of *The Divine Comedy*. Materially, it implies that the events of the soul that constitute romantic love can and do shape themselves so as to be isomorphic with the gospel narrative. The beloved, as Williams puts it, 'becomes the Mother of Love; Love is born in the soul; it may have its passion there; it may have its resurrection there. It has its own divine nature united with our undivine nature.'[19] In the lover as in Judæa the pattern of the glory becomes incarnate. Two natures unite, as they did and do in Christ; and, as in Christ, this incarnation takes place, not by a conver-sion of deity into flesh, but by a taking of humanity into God.

These high claims about romantic love stop short of a claim to ex-clusive validity. There are other means of access to 'a state of *caritas* of the utmost possible height and breadth', other languages for ascribing to matter the significance and power it has in the light of the Incarnation. 'Romantic love between the sexes is', Williams allows, 'but one kind of romantic love, which is but a particular habit of Romanticism as a whole, which is itself but a particular method of the Affirmation of Images.' Ultimately, because it is the almost incredible nature of things that no fact is excluded from the glory of God, there is no fact of which it is impossible to say, 'This also is Thou'. In Dante the fact affirmed is a Florentine girl, who 'was, in her degree, an image of nobility, of virtue, of the Redeemed Life, in some sense of Almighty God himself'.[20] Yet the meaning of the affirmation is not that Beatrice was *like* nobility, virtue, the redeemed life, the Almighty. She was like nothing but herself. It was for just that reason – because she was entirely and exclusively the person she was and no other – that she could be an image. And it is for the same reason, no other, that any other fact functions, if it does, as an image in Williams's sense of the word.

Events of the soul, romantic love among them, find expression in Williams's novels through narratives of his own invention. His romantic theology, which expounds the relation of such events to the received narrative that defines Christianity, thus stands as a kind of bridge from his fiction to the theological writings that examine and interpret this narrative in its own right. Like the novels, Williams's reading of the Gospels is highly personal, in the sense that it bespeaks a unique and individual cast of mind. In the sense of relying on or appealing to sentiment, there is scarcely anything personal about it, least of all in his strikingly impersonal portrait (if 'portrait' is the right word) of Jesus. In some sense Williams was not much interested in Jesus. At least, he seldom uses that (personal) name. Even the title 'Christ' appears in his writing less frequently than 'Messias', spelled according to the Greek, as in the King James Bible. 'Christ', he points out, makes its first abrupt appearance in the earliest Gospel narrative as 'a kind of incantation, the invocation of a ritual, antique, and magical title . . .'[21] Now that these associations are thoroughly worn off, the somewhat antique form of a somewhat unusual equivalent helps to make the point that Williams is most concerned to make: by whatever name or title he is designated, the protagonist of the Gospels is strange.

The point is developed most effectively in a chapter of *He Came Down from Heaven* that is as brilliant as anything Williams wrote.

Commentaries, scholarly or devotional, generally make for dull reading. To read the Gospels in the light of Williams's comments is to be confronted with a story more vivid, more urgent and above all more enigmatic than standard interpretations are likely to suggest. He examines the text, as he does the rest of the Bible, 'by the methods of literary criticism, by the contemplation of the states of being the book describes, by the relation of phrase to phrase and the illumination of phrase by phrase, by the discovery (without ingenuity) of complexity within complexity and simplicity within simplicity. There is simply no other way to go about it, because it consists of words.'[22] These are not much like the methods commonly deployed in quests for the historical Jesus. Williams's approach does not begin with the idea, which questers seem to take for granted, that behind the words and phrases as we have them there must be a man who was not much like what the words and phrases say and not much different from us. Far from disintegrating the text, Williams takes it as it stands. Far from sidelining its apocalyptic features, he underscores them. Far from piecing together a plausible personality for the main character, he speaks of that character as 'the Divine Thing' and uses neuter pronouns.

For this last peculiarity there is, as Williams notes, a precedent in the King James translation, though hardly a strong one.[23] Be that as it may, the effect of reading it again and again is disconcerting, as it was no doubt intended to be. In much the same way that the style of Williams's novels discourages quick and superficial reading, his discussion of the Gospel narrative is written so as to subvert the familiarity of the narrative discussed. 'Divine Thing', like 'Messias', plays a part in accentuating the otherness of the story and above all the otherness of what 'came down from heaven'. Williams by no means denies that, in Christ, God has been made altogether like us. That is the doctrine of the Incarnation. Nor does he discount the love and gratitude which this likeness has evoked. He does hold that there is at least an 'equal satisfaction that it is an *unlike* us who is so made. It is an alien Power which is caught and suspended in our very midst.'[24] In emphasizing the unlikeness of this Other, this 'alien Power', Williams is counteracting the perennial temptation to domesticate it, intellectually or otherwise. The Incarnation certainly means, among other things, that 'any human energy . . . is capable of being assumed into sacramental and transcendental heights'.[25] But the operative word is 'assumed'. The Incarnation did not take place 'by conversion of the Godhead into flesh'. That would be, by definition, magic. It took place 'by taking of the manhood into God'. So and not otherwise are any human energies – sexual, scholarly, imaginative, political – subsumed into the 'pattern of the Glory'.

The union of diverse natures, of sensuality and substance, of human and divine, in the single Person of Messias is the cause and exemplar of all 'taking of the manhood into God'. As such, the Incarnation also exemplifies the principle that Williams called *co-inherence*. The word is almost a trademark, so thoroughly does the idea it names animate all that he wrote. He borrowed it from the theology of the Trinity, where co-inherence names the supreme mystery that Dante tries to describe at the very end of *The Divine Comedy*: the way in which each of the three divine Persons includes the other two, living in them and through them without ceasing to be distinct. That, for a divine Person, is what it is to *be* – to exist reciprocally, in mutual communication and interrelatedness, and to have a personal identity wholly constituted by those relations. What a human person is to be is, in its degree, the same: being-from, being-in, being-for an other. Co-inherence, which in God is an eternal fact, is in men and women a natural, or anyhow a naturally possible, fact. These facts converge 'at the meeting of two heavenward lines, one drawn from Bethany along the Ascent of Messias, the other from Jerusalem against the Descent of the Paraclete'.[26] In that intersection a third, supernatural fact began: Christendom, the kingdom, the co-inherence of the Holy Spirit and humankind in, and as, the history of the Church. This co-inherent organism is the subject of Williams's book *The Descent of the Dove*, which has been called the only imaginative Church history ever written. It exemplifies, on a wider scale, the same illuminatingly eccentric approach and style as *He Came Down from Heaven*. But co-inherence consists, like the glory of God, in facts, and the relevant facts need not be vast historical movements such as the ones that Williams names 'the renewal of contrition' and 'the reconciliation with time'. Equally, they may be events that happen in the soul.

One of these events is the exchange of roles and acts and experiences that Williams includes under the rubric of substitution. Traditional theology is here again the source of the term; specifically, the theology of the Atonement and 'the substitution, in the last experiences, of our sacred Lord for us'.[27] To this 'vertical' exchange corresponds the 'horizontal' exchange summed up in the New Testament precept 'bear ye one another's burdens'. The precept is to be followed literally, in Williams's judgment, and applied to burdens that may be more and other than physical. To carry someone else's fear, that is, may be no less possible, and no less needful, than to carry someone else's groceries. As with romantic love, 'the thing happens'. Williams recommends it so often and so earnestly as to suggest that the thing had happened to him, and that he knew at first hand what he was recommending. It is in one of his novels, however, that he gives his richest account of this specific kind of substitution, and only a long quotation will do to convey its specificity. It describes the experience of Peter Stanhope, a character who is a poet, a playwright, and perhaps something of Williams himself in other ways as well. Stanhope has learned from a neighbour, Pauline by name, that she has occasionally met with a *Doppelgänger*, an exact double of herself, and lives in constant terror of another such encounter. Has she never, Stanhope enquires, asked a friend to carry this fear for her? She has not. He volunteers, as courteously as Williams might have done, to carry it himself. Pauline agrees, a little sceptically, to let him try, and as she leaves to walk home, he settles himself to do so:

A certain superficial attention, alert and effective in its degree, lay at the disposal of anyone who might need it, exactly as his body was prepared to draw in its long outstretched legs if anyone wanted to pass. Meanwhile he disposed the rest of his attention according to his promise. He recollected Pauline; he visualized her going along a road, any road; he visualized another Pauline coming to meet her. As he did so his mind contemplated not the first but the second Pauline; he took trouble to apprehend the vision, he summoned through all his sensations an approaching fear. Deliberately he opened himself to that fear, laying aside for awhile every thought of why he was doing it, forgetting every principle and law, absorbing only the strangeness and the terror of that separate spiritual identity.... He sat on, imagining to himself the long walk with its sinister possibility, the ogreish world lying around, the air with its treachery to all sane appearance. His own eyes began to seek and strain and shrink, his own feet, quiet though actually they were, began to weaken with the necessity of advance upon the road down which the girl was passing. The body of his flesh received her alien terror, his mind carried the burden of her world. The burden was inevitably lighter for him than for her, for the rage of a personal resentment was lacking. He endured her sensitiveness, but not her sin;

the substitution there, if indeed there is a substitution, is hidden in the central mystery of Christendom which Christendom itself has never understood, nor can.[28]

Meanwhile Pauline arrives at home, startled by the realization that, for the first time in years, she has walked the whole way without ever dreading the thought that her *Doppelgänger* might appear.

Williams makes a point of saying in the novel that it is irrelevant whether the apparition that had terrified Pauline was an actual being or a figment. Either way, her terror was an actual burden, actually borne and felt and undergone by another in her place. The passage itself makes two further points. In describing this event of substitution Williams associates it with 'the central mystery of Christendom', the suffering of Christ on behalf of others. In the same way that he regarded the Incarnation as embracing in itself every other 'taking of the manhood into God', so too he held that in 'the Divine Substitution of Messias' all forms of exchange and substitution are included.[29] There is, however, a difference. At the end of the passage quoted, Williams distinguishes between sensitiveness and resentful rage. Both pertain to events in the soul. The second, he implies, is sin, but not the first; the first, but not the second, allows of exchange and substitution between ordinary human friends. If Williams had been a less careful writer, it would be rash to draw from these lines any conclusion about his theological position. In fact, what he suggests here is entirely consistent with the conception of sin developed in his non-fictional writings. It is a remarkable conception, to say the least.

Williams sometimes refers to sin as a 'chosen catastrophe'. The catastrophe needs no argument; the facts of present human existence exhibit it. There is, however, an authorized explication of the choice, set out near the beginning of Genesis. It is commonly called the story of the Fall. Williams calls it 'the myth of the alteration in knowledge'. By 'myth' he intends no antithesis to history; 'history is itself a myth; to the imaginative, engaged in considering these things, all is equally myth'.[30] And in any case the catastrophe has not stopped happening; that is why it is catastrophic. 'The definition of the Fall is that man determined to know good as evil.'[31] Alter the verb by inserting 'is' before 'determined', and the meaning remains the same.

That is the conclusion that Williams draws by applying his own brand of literary criticism to the tale in Genesis. Three points, in his judgment, stand out. First, eating the 'fruit of the tree' would, sup-posedly, bring an enlargement of knowledge, a knowledge of good *and* evil. Second, to have this enlarged knowledge would be to know differently, to know 'as gods'. Third, this godlike mode of knowing was forbidden to the man and the woman – to 'the Adam', as Williams puts it, meaning the co-inherent totality of humankind, which at this point in Genesis consists of two. It was thus known to the Adam that there was a knowledge above and beyond their own, that obtaining it would be disaster, and that refusing it belonged to the good which was their relationship to the creator. Why was this further knowledge not permitted? Because, Williams proposes, it was not possible. Had it been a possibility for the Adam to know 'as gods', it would not have been forbidden. It was not a possibility. God, whose knowing is by sheer intelligence, can know good not only in itself but in its depriv-ation. Otherwise stated, it is possible for God to know evil without, by knowing it, bringing the deprivation – the evil – into existence. The same was and is impossible for the Adam, whose knowing was and is experiential. Nevertheless, it was this impossibility that they wanted. They wanted to know a schism in the universe, a negation of the good they already knew. They wanted to know evil as well as good. 'Since there was not – since there never has been and never will be – anything else than the good to know, they knew the good as antagonism.' What they had wanted to know, they could not possibly know as God knows it, by intellect alone, so they knew it in the only way that was, for them, a possibility; they knew evil in the same way that they already knew the good, that is, by experience. 'They had what they wanted. That they did not like it when they got it does not alter the fact that they certainly got it.'[32]

Such, in Williams's account, is the catastrophic alteration of human knowing. 'The definition of the Fall is that man determined to know good as evil.' To know it so, experientially, is an absurdity, a contradic-tion, a cognitive, moral, imaginative lie. Choosing the contradiction deprives some good of its being, some being of its good. In so doing, the choice generates (not to say creates) its own object; that is, it constitutes an evil. Since what is so constituted is a fact, it is per-mitted, 'under the Mercy', to exist. Yet at the same time it remains true that 'the glory of God is in facts'. Somehow, therefore, evil must have a 'reason' for being, some place or purpose in the pattern of the glory that includes all facts. Williams is not interested in the abstract problem of theodicy, although he has a good deal to say about the book of Job. He is, however, interested in asking what it is that evil, since it does exist, exists *for*. His answer is that evil exists to be forgiven.

Forgiveness assumes in Williams's later writings a prominence that romantic love has in the earlier. On forgiveness he wrote his last non-fiction book, and it is the leitmotiv in *All Hallows' Eve*, his last novel. Forgiveness is one form, the deepest form, of bearing one another's burdens. 'All difference consists in the mode of knowledge',[33] and since sin is knowing the good, deliberately and experientially, as evil, so likewise forgiveness is knowing experienced evil differently – knowing it as good, as an occasion for good, as a means to good. To forgive is not to forget, the adage notwithstanding, although forgetting may do as a temporary expedient. To forgive, in the most serious sense, is precisely to *remember* – in a certain way. Forgotten facts are not undone, as though history could be made to run backwards. What has happened did happen. The important question, as with romantic love, is what happens next.

That depends, not on whether but on *how* a sin is remembered. There can be, Williams writes, 'only two attitudes towards the sin of another towards oneself; one is to entertain a grudge, the other is not to entertain a grudge'.[34] Each is an event of the soul, a way of remembering. To entertain a grudge is to prolong the injury, to extend its life by nursing it with the feelings it feeds on. Such is the 'rage of a personal resentment' mentioned in the account of Peter Stanhope's substitution. On the other hand, *not* to entertain a grudge is to invert Adam's decision, to know 'after the mode of heaven', to re-identify oneself with the good. Forgiveness as Williams construes it is a full awareness of sin, in love. The reversal of offence, that is to say, is effected in and by the offended, the 'innocent' party.

This is a hard saying, one of Williams's hardest. It assaults an intuitive sense of justice, a feeling that (in all fairness) sin ought to be undone, put right, by the sinner, the 'guilty' party. Just so, Williams would reply; but forgiveness is not a matter of all fairness. Forgiveness stands to justice as does the Incarnation of the kingdom to its Precursor. In the Gospels it is John the Baptist who takes up the prophets' passionate call for justice, whereas the sayings of the Incarnate, as Williams reads them, 'make it impossible for a child of the kingdom, for a Christian, to talk of justice or injustice so far as he personally is concerned'.[35] What concerns the Christian, precisely as Christian, is the forgiveness of sins, which is a function not of desert and obligation but of substitution; ultimately, a substitution 'hidden in the central mystery of Christendom'. It is starting on the wrong foot to ask who has contracted a legitimate debt because of illegitimate absurdity, for the question supposes that sinner and sinned-against, offender and offended, are separate existences. Suppose, instead, that they are not; suppose that they exist co-inherently, each in the other. In that case, what matters is that repentance and forgiveness should occur, and deciding who ought (in all fairness) to bear the burden of repenting or forgiving is secondary. 'The guilty repents; the as greatly guilty forgives; there is therefore but one maxim for both: "make haste".'[36] The very distinction between repenting and forgiving fades; they become aspects of one shared state of mind, explicitly identified when Williams writes of 'the consciousness of repentance – that is, the consciousness of sin in love; that is, of the forgiveness of sin'.[37]

* * *

It is curious that while Williams uses the word 'image' constantly, 'imagination' is rare. His writings say a great deal about particular images – the image of the city, the Beatrician image of the beloved, the image of the human body – but hardly anything about an inventive, 'creative' capacity called imagination. The reason is partly that an image, in Williams's sense, is not primarily a visual presentation – or, if it is, the meaning that belongs to it is a worded meaning, 'built up by many descriptions, similes, metaphors, and maxims'.[38] That is why the cinematic version of a Williams novel, however admirable as cinema, would not communicate all, or even very much, of what Williams meant. He was building intellectual patterns, not painting verbal pictures. Even the most fantastically imaginative passages in his novels are informed by a passion for precision, definition and order.

As for imagination itself, the mental power or faculty, there is little to suggest that Williams thought of it as affording a privileged access to the glory of God. Still less does it generate the facts in which that glory consists. On its own, imagination is as likely as not to generate counterfeits and illusions. If there is a character in Williams's fiction who can be said to be endowed with a fertile imagination, it is the self-damned historian Wentworth, whose moral and metaphysical descent into hell is described, terrifyingly, in the novel so named. It is Wentworth who brings a 'fact' into being – a succubus, a factitious other, a lover all his own, wholly amenable to the desires of its maker, provided that the real, factual woman of whom it is a simulacrum remains out of sight and out of mind.

W. H. Auden, whose admiration for Williams knew no bounds, was perhaps thinking of this episode when he wrote the section of his long Christmas poem *For the Time Being* called 'The Meditation of Simeon'. Into this extended reflection on the Incarnation, Auden appears to have absorbed several characteristic themes of Williams's theology. In the present context, one sentence in particular stands out. Speaking of the newborn Christ, Simeon says: 'Because in Him the Flesh is united to the Word without magical transformation, Imagination is redeemed from promiscuous fornication with her own images.'[39] Williams would concur. It is not imagination as such but imagination as redeemed that has a place in 'the pattern of the glory'. For to redeemed imagination images are not self-generated phantasms: they are embodied accuracies, worded and regulated and set in order by the 'taking of the manhood into God' that is the Incarnation of the Word.

Notes

1 C. S. Lewis, preface to *Essays Presented to Charles Williams*, ed. C. S. Lewis (London: Oxford University Press, 1947), p. vii.

2 T. S. Eliot, introduction to Charles Williams, *All Hallows' Eve* (New York: Pellegrini & Cudahy, 1948), p. xi.

3 Charles Williams, 'The Productions of Time', *Time and Tide* 22 (25 January 1941), pp. 72–3.

4 Jared Lobdell, ed., *The Detective Fiction Reviews of Charles Williams, 1930–1935* (Jefferson, NC, and London: McFarland, 2003); see esp. pp. 15–16.

5 Charles Williams, *The Greater Trumps* (1932; repr., New York: Pellegrini & Cudahy, 1950), p. 110.

6 Charles Williams, *The Descent of the Dove: A Short History of the Holy Spirit in the Church* (1939; repr., Grand Rapids, MI: Eerdmans, 1968), p. 58.

7 William Lindsay Gresham, preface to Williams, *The Greater Trumps*, p. ix. Gresham was the first husband of Joy Davidman, who was later married to C. S. Lewis.

8 See for example Charles Williams, *He Came Down from Heaven/The Forgiveness of Sins* (London: Faber and Faber, 1950), p. 161.

9 Charles Williams, 'Natural Goodness', in *The Image of the City, and Other Essays*, ed. Anne Ridler (London: Oxford University Press, 1958), p. 79. This and 'The Redeemed City', 'St John', 'The Way of Affirmation' (as 'The Church Looks Forward'), 'The Cross' and 'Natural Goodness' are also available in *Charles Williams: Essential Writings in Spirituality and Theology*, ed. Charles Hefling (Cambridge, MA: Cowley, 1993).

10 Eliot, Introduction, in Williams, *All Hallows' Eve*, p. xv.

11 Williams, *He Came Down/Forgiveness*, p. 33.

12 Charles Williams, 'The Redeemed City', in *The Image of the City*, p. 110.

13 Dorothy L. Sayers, 'Dante and Charles Williams', in *The Whimsical Christian* (New York: Macmillan, 1978), p. 185.

14 Williams, *He Came Down/Forgiveness*, p. 36.

15 Williams, *He Came Down/Forgiveness*, p. 66.

16 Notably by Mary McDermott Shideler in *The Theology of Romantic Love: A Study in the Writings of Charles Williams* (New York: Harper, 1962).

17 Williams, *He Came Down/Forgiveness*, p. 77.

18 Charles Williams, 'St John', in *The Image of the City*, p. 88.

19 Williams, *He Came Down/Forgiveness*, p. 81.

20 Charles Williams, *The Figure of Beatrice* (1943; repr., Berkeley: Apocryphile, 2005), pp. 7–8.

21 Williams, *He Came Down/Forgiveness*, p. 51.

22 Williams, *He Came Down/Forgiveness*, p. 15.

23 Luke 1.35 AV, 'that holy thing'; Williams, *He Came Down/Forgiveness*, p. 49.

24 Charles Williams, 'The Cross', in *The Image of the City*, p. 137; emphasis added.

25 Charles Williams, *Outlines of Romantic Theology*, ed. Mary Alice Hadfield (Grand Rapids, MI: Eerdmans, 1990), p. 9.

26 Williams, *The Descent of the Dove*, p. 1.

27 Charles Williams, 'The Way of Affirmation', in *The Image of the City*, p. 158.

28 Charles Williams, *Descent into Hell* (Grand Rapids, MI: Eerdmans, 1999), pp. 100–1.

29 See the 'constitution' that Williams drew up for the Order of the Co-Inherence, in *Charles Williams: Essential Writings*, pp. 149–50, item 6.

30 Charles Williams, 'The Figure of Arthur', in *Taliessin through Logres, The Region of the Summer Stars, and Arthurian Torso* (Grand Rapids, MI: Eerdmans, 1974), p. 264.

31 Charles Williams, 'Natural Goodness', in *The Image of the City*, p. 77.

32 Williams, *He Came Down/Forgiveness*, p. 21.
33 Williams, *He Came Down/Forgiveness*, p. 21.
34 Charles Williams, 'Blake and Wordsworth', in *The Image of the City*, p. 66.
35 Williams, *He Came Down/Forgiveness*, p. 53.
36 Williams, *He Came Down/Forgiveness*, p. 198.
37 Williams, *He Came Down/Forgiveness*, p. 151.
38 Charles Williams, 'The Image of the City in English Verse', in *The Image of the City*, p. 92.
39 W. H. Auden, *For the Time Being: A Christmas Oratorio*, in *Collected Longer Poems* (New York: Random House, 1969), p. 182.

Figure 5 Rose Macaulay.
National Portrait Gallery, London.

5

Rose Macaulay: A voice from the edge

DAVID HEIN

A voice from the edge

In 1956 Rose Macaulay applied the alchemy of her art to material drawn from her own experience – as professional writer, international traveller, illicit lover and religious pilgrim – and produced an unusual book called *The Towers of Trebizond*. Representing the culmination of a long and successful career, this novel garnered plaudits from all quarters. Macaulay's peers in the literary realm awarded it the James Tait Black Memorial Prize for 1957. And in January 1958, on the recommendation of Prime Minister Harold Macmillan, the Queen included Macaulay in the New Year's Honours List, making her a Dame Commander of the British Empire.

The recognition that gave Rose Macaulay the most satisfaction, however, came from her fellow travellers on the Christian way, who told her that this novel had had a positive effect on their spiritual lives. Many clergy and laity found their faith reinvigorated by reading her book. Macaulay wrote to her sister that 'A young woman I didn't know came up to me at the Empire Hall & told me reading *Trebizond* at a crucial moment in her life had decided her for the right course . . . [There have also been] clergy who read bits of it to doubting ordinands, with successful results.'[1] Written, she recalled, 'in a kind of white-hot passion',[2] this novel was 'meant to be about the struggle of good and evil, its eternal importance, and the power of the Christian Church over the soul, to torment and convert'.[3]

That a book which appears to have more to do with the Church's capacity 'to torment' than with its power to 'convert' should produce such 'successful results' is remarkable in itself. The paradox of its popular reception by Christians and would-be believers is part of the mystery of *The Towers of Trebizond*. An answer to this conundrum may lie in the way in which this novel engages the reader's heart and mind. The story presents dilemmas and reveals their attractions, but it declines to provide stock solutions. The text is realistically unstable; it throws out a question for each apparent answer. 'Determinedly anti-romantic to the last', comments one literary scholar, Macaulay 'blended causticity and piety into a heady modern brew.' Hers is 'an art of contrarieties played against each other'.[4]

No doubt the capacity of twentieth-century Anglicanism to handle contrarieties increased Rose Macaulay's appreciation of this branch of the Church Catholic. She wrote *Trebizond* after her return to the Anglican fold, but in this work of fiction she does not presume to mark out for her readers the steps on the journey of faith which only they could take. The novel's ending is gratifyingly indeterminate, reassuring in its refusals.

In relation to some of the best-known spiritual guides of her era, Rose Macaulay occupied a position on the rim. She was neither altogether within nor completely outside the circle of C. S. Lewis, Austin Farrer and other well-known Christian apologists of her day. She appears not only to have read but also to have known nearly all of them. For example, in one of her published letters, she mentions meeting C. S. Lewis at St Francis' House, London: 'He is very good and quick and witty in public speech, and I enjoyed him. It was my part to stimulate him with questions, and the evening went quite well. He is a great influence among the undergraduates.'[5]

Lewis mentions her by name in *Letters to Malcolm*. In a discussion of the merits of prayers written by others versus prayers of one's own composition, Lewis talks about Macaulay as a determined collector of the former. He tells Malcolm that he was 'staggered' but not 'repelled' by Macaulay's habit of searching for and relying upon '"ready-made" prayers'. And he notes that he'd 'had . . . the luck to meet her'. 'Make no mistake,' he assures the reader of his letter. 'She was the right sort; one of the most fully civilised people I ever knew.'[6]

Macaulay was also acquainted with Austin Farrer. In the 1950s, she was a frequent visitor to St Anne's House, Dean Street, in London. St Anne's House was a centre for spiritual formation which featured lectures and discussions on religious topics. Farrer was among the Anglican luminaries who lectured there. On a visit to Oxford in June 1951, Macaulay had sherry with Farrer, who was then chaplain of Trinity College. She had earlier read his Bampton Lectures, *The Glass of Vision*, finding them interesting but hard to follow.[7]

Macaulay knew another St Anne's House lecturer besides Austin Farrer: Dorothy L. Sayers. The Sayers scholar Barbara Reynolds has made a strong case for seeing an important character in *The Towers of Trebizond*, Aunt Dot, as 'an affectionate take-off of' Dorothy L. Sayers. Reynolds thinks it possible that the strong, practical words that Aunt Dot addresses to Laurie (quoted on p. 98) were words that Sayers spoke to Rose Macaulay – in which case the portrait of Sayers in the novel 'may be seen as an affectionate gesture of gratitude'. Reynolds points out that Macaulay was one of only eight persons invited to the ceremony in 1958 at which Sayers's ashes were placed under the floor of the tower of St Anne's Church.[8]

There is another sense in which Rose Macaulay held a place on the circumference of this circle of prominent Christian writers. While she certainly was, as Judith Moore has noted, 'one of the few significant English novelists of the twentieth century to identify herself as a Christian and to use Christian themes in her writing', Macaulay was never a simple believer in mere Christianity.[9] During the 1930s and 1940s, when such writers as Lewis, Farrer and Sayers were publishing books that were both imaginative and consistently orthodox, Macaulay was a lapsed Anglican, alienated from the Church. Even after her return to the faith in 1950–1, in *The Towers of Trebizond* she produced a novel the heroine of which, to some extent a stand-in for her creator, occupies terrain at or beyond the Christian border.

Macaulay knew this territory well. On her journey of faith, doubt was a steady companion. The hydraulics of her spiritual life were such that throughout her last years, when she was to all appearances a practising Christian of deep piety, she remained sceptical about much that the tradition deemed essential; just as, throughout her long period as an 'Anglo-agnostic', she was never certain of her unbelief, or free of spiritual guilt, or unable to appreciate a good sermon. Macaulay's best fiction reflects the divisions that can afflict the modern soul.

For today's Christians, who may be accustomed to reading spiritual books that are safely traditional and mildly escapist, Macaulay presents an intriguing alternative. *Trebizond* offers the story of an Englishwoman named Laurie – age about 35 – who attracts the reader's interest through the winsomeness of her character and holds the reader's attention through the appeal of her struggle. Her personality is uniquely her own, while her situation is both individual and common. Like other religious questers in nineteenth- and twentieth-century fiction, such as John Updike's Harry ('Rabbit') Angstrom, Laurie is both a solitary figure and a corporate personality.

As Sir Philip Sidney declared in his *Defense of Poesy* (1595), the literary artist 'couples the general notion with the particular example'.[10] While philosophers are restricted to abstract generalizations and historians are tied to concrete facts, poets – by 'poets' Sidney meant all those who display imaginative power in their writing – are free to exercise their imaginations and to produce work that brings together the particular and the universal. Literary artists thereby avoid the limitations and retain the virtues of both philosophers and historians.[11] Laurie is not only a captivating individual in her own right but also a universal: in her plight we recognize aspects of our own condition.

Outside the shimmering towers of Trebizond

A modern young woman who retains a reverence for tradition, Laurie comes across as thoughtful and conscientious, despite her flaws. Early in the novel she sets out on a missionary journey to Turkey in the company of two eccentrics: her Aunt Dot and an Anglo-Catholic priest named Father Chantry-Pigg. The former is 'a cheerful and romantic adventuress'.[12] The latter is a religious fundamentalist who is 'better at condemning than at loving' (p. 28).

Possessing a deeply ambivalent attitude toward the Church, Laurie is better at loving than at praying: her affair with a married man has kept her away from the Church of England for ten years. 'From time to time', she says, 'I knew what I had lost. But nearly all the time, God was a bad second, enough to hurt but not to cure, to hide from but not to seek' (p. 65). She acknowledges the other pole of her ambivalence toward Christianity when she remarks that, although 'the Church met its Waterloo . . . when I took up with adultery', Anglicanism was still 'in the system', and, once in, 'I think one cannot get it out' (p. 66).

What holds Laurie back from a fully committed Christian faith is, in large measure, her attachment to her lover, Vere. He is amusing, smart and attractive (p. 268). When she is with him, she falls into a 'doped oblivion', an intoxication that shuts down 'conscience and the moral sense' (p. 184). Whatever misgivings about deeper involvement she had early on are soon allayed by the growing sense of peace and happiness that the romance gives her. With the commencement of their affair, each year together is 'better than the one before, love and joy gradually drowning remorse' (p. 273). Thus Laurie finds herself in a moral fog, no longer sure what sin is, hesitating to pray because 'I did not really want to be saved from my sins, not for the time being, it would make things too difficult and too sad' (p. 150).

The reader learns, however, that Laurie's Augustine-echoing resistance to being delivered just yet is only one of the reasons behind her disinclination to rejoin the Church. There are also the faults of Christian institutions down the centuries. At one point in the story she feels that 'what was keeping me from the Church was not my own sins but those of the Church' (p. 178). She observes how the Church 'grew so far, almost at once, from anything which can have been intended'. It 'became . . . blood-stained and persecuting and cruel and war-like and made small and trivial things so important' (p. 196).

Laurie's objections are intellectual as well as moral. The Church, she says, began 'with a magnificent idea', but that idea had 'to be worked out by human beings who do not understand much of it but interpret it in their own way and think they are guided by God, whom they have not yet grasped' (p. 196). She questions the historicity of the Gospel accounts: 'I wonder what was really said, how far the evangelists got it right, and how much they left out, writing it down long after.' No inerrantist, she is aware that 'some of the things they forgot and left out might have been very important, and some of the things they put in they perhaps got wrong, for some sound unlikely for [Jesus] to have said' (p. 203).

Laurie sees that 'no Church can have more than a very little of the truth', and therefore she finds it impossible 'to believe, as some people do, that one's Church has all the truth and no errors, for how could this possibly be?' She realizes that while it 'must be comfortable and reassuring' to think that one's own denomination – she mentions Roman Catholics, Anglicans and Calvinists – has 'the faith once for all delivered to the saints', 'most of us know that nothing is as true as all that . . . for new things are being discovered all the time, and old things dropped, like the whole Bible being true, and we have to grope our way through a mist that keeps being lit by shafts of light, so that exploration tends to be patchy' (p. 226).

That the barriers to religious commitment include more than the impediment of her adultery becomes apparent in the final chapter of the book when Vere is killed and Laurie still cannot re-enter the Church. At this point in the narrative, the rollicking features of the story fall by the wayside, and the novel turns deadly serious. Back in London, Laurie is at the wheel of the car in which Vere dies; her pride and impetuosity cause her to reject her lover's caution and to assert her rights against a bus that has crashed a red light. Now, without Vere, Laurie feels that she must live 'in two hells, for I have lost God' and lost, too, 'the love I want' (p. 276).

Aunt Dot – who does sound a bit like Dorothy L. Sayers – hopes that her niece will make her peace with the Church, now that the way is open to her (p. 274). She tells Laurie: 'I think, my dear, . . . the Church used once to be an opiate to you . . . You dramatized it and yourself, you felt carried along in something aesthetically exciting and beautiful and romantic; you were a dilettante, escapist Anglican.' She offers her niece some practical advice: 'One mustn't lose sight of the hard core, which is, do this, do that, love your friends and like your neighbours, be just, be extravagantly generous, be honest, be tolerant, have courage, have compassion, use your wits and your imagination, . . . don't dramatize and dream and escape.' 'That', Aunt Dot tells her, 'seems to me to be the pattern, so far as we can make it out here. So come in again with your eyes open, when you feel you can' (pp. 274–5). 'But', Laurie declares, 'I did not feel that I could' (p. 275).

In this novel, 'Trebizond' is not simply the old name for Trabzon, a port in northeastern Turkey on the shores of the Black Sea. Trebizond is the 'fabled city' that Laurie feels cut off from (p. 276). In the thirteenth and fourteenth centuries, Trebizond was a great artistic and trading centre; its prominence derived from its position at the heart of the commercial route through Asia Minor. This city was 'fabled' not only because of its former splendour but also because it did not fall to Sultan Mehmet II until 1461, eight years after the Turkish conquest of Constantinople. It was renowned, then, as the final refuge of Hellenistic civilization. In Macaulay's novel, 'Trebizond' can be read as symbolizing the Christian faith or the Church. The author herself said that 'Trebizond stands for not merely the actual city (tho' this comes in, and a lovely place it is) but for the ideal and romantic and nostalgic vision of the Church which haunts the person who narrates the story.'[13]

The Towers of Trebizond, which begins on a famously jaunty note, ends on a note of despair. For Laurie, the towers of Trebizond 'shimmer on a far horizon, gated and walled and held in a luminous enchantment. It seems that for me . . . this must for ever be. But at the city's heart lie the pattern and the hard core, and these I can never make my own: they are too far outside my range. The pattern should be easier, the core less hard. This seems, indeed, the eternal dilemma' (pp. 275–6).

Rose Macaulay assured readers dismayed by her book's gloomy ending that her central character would not always find Trebizond so inaccessible. To her spiritual advisor, Father Hamilton Johnson, Macaulay wrote these words of comfort: 'Yes, the *Times Literary Supplement* reviewer . . . took me to be more "in the dark" than I am. Laurie *was*, of course, still, when the book ends. So, once, was I. Laurie will come later on to where I am now, give her time.'[14]

But interpreting Laurie's later moves by expanding the narrative and stretching out its timeline beyond the published text is a dubious business. After all, Laurie does not exist except as a character within the pages of this novel. And before we uncritically accept the author's opinions regarding her heroine's future, we might pause to consider D. H. Lawrence's caution to 'Trust the tale', not the artist.[15] Taken on its own terms, as a discrete work of art, *Trebizond* ends with its main character sounding thoroughly dejected, as she affirms the difficulty of the pattern and the unyielding hardness of the core.[16] Understandably, Macaulay's sister Jean called this book 'a story of utter failure and despair'.[17] Which brings us to the paradox mentioned in the first section of this chapter. As one literary scholar has put the matter, 'It is the highest of ironies that a novel which ends on such a note of – perhaps even unchristian? – despair should be hailed as one of the twentieth century's most luminous Christian novels.'[18]

One way of reading this book which might suggest a more optimistic view of its ending is to see Laurie's situation as that of a person who has 'initial faith' but not yet full faith. Austin Farrer defined initial faith as a way station on the road to a more settled Christian conviction. It is, he wrote in *Saving Belief*, 'that attitude of openness or responsiveness through which we move towards an acknowledgement of God's existence'.[19] Those with 'initial faith' are attracted by Christian faith but find themselves unable to commit. The Christian life of faith sparks their interest, but they remain divided.[20] At the end of this novel much still restrains Laurie from moving toward the shimmering towers of Trebizond, and it is impossible to say in which direction she will eventually turn. But it is important to acknowledge the pre-faith that she already has, and Farrer's concept helps us with this perception. At the very least, the language that Laurie uses to express her religious yearning indicates that she is keenly aware of what she is missing, and that sense is a major element in what Farrer means by initial faith.

Another way of reading this book which might shift our view of its ending is to comprehend Laurie's character less in diachronic than in synchronic terms. Instead of imagining her moving along a historical timeline from unbelief through initial faith to, possibly, full faith – that is, from past through present to a projected future – we can try to grasp the various elements in her make-up as we know them from studying her character throughout the book. When we do, we find hints of something more at work in her than initial faith only.

Keeping in mind these additional elements, we may come to suspect that the definitive foreclosing of possibilities dramatically announced on the novel's last page – 'the pattern and the hard core . . . these I can never make my own' – is more apparent than real. We may see that, considered in relation to all that has gone before, Laurie's dispirited, once-for-all rejection of the consolations of faith is rooted less in her actual nature and more in the immediate trauma of the death of her lover: deprived of love, she is also bereft of hope. Viewed against a larger backdrop, the ending may seem more ambiguous and therefore less bleak than it at first appears.

Laurie's description of some of the Church's failings has been mentioned. She speaks of what happens when 'a magnificent idea' is worked out by human beings over centuries: the Church's leaders manage to lose much that is of value, they add much that is irrelevant, and they think that all the time they are guided by the Holy Spirit. We should note, however, that in this same passage Laurie goes on to say that these frequently wayward, uncomprehending, self-righteous Christians should not be entirely dismissed either, for 'they had grasped something' (p. 196).

What had they grasped? In a conversation that she has in Jerusalem with a sceptical acquaintance named David, Laurie searches for an answer. After telling him that she hasn't got the answers and that he should take his questions to the bishop, she suggests he 'read some of the liturgies and missals'. Like a good Anglican, she reaches into liturgy for her answer. Her reply comes by way of the Great Antiphons. Composed by Benedictine monks in the early sixth century, they were recited during the seven days leading to the Christmas Vigil. Laurie quotes for David the Advent hymns to the divine wisdom (*O Sapientia*) and to the divine light (*O Oriens* [O Dawn of the East]). She thereby suggests that these ancient liturgies contain treasures worthy of notice. The Great Antiphons point to the divine wisdom of which the major traditions contain only pieces and to the eternal light that the world's religions reflect in broken lights and mended lives (p. 199).[21]

To Laurie, David has posed a challenge the force of which she feels as well: How can a thoughtful person hold that this elaborate system of doctrine, liturgy and ecclesiastical offices is consonant with the intentions of the historical Jesus, 'this young Jew in Palestine'? Laurie answers by urging David to focus instead on 'the light of the spirit, the light that has lighted every man who came into the world'. She directs his gaze away from the scandalous particular to the meaningful universal: 'What I mean is, it wasn't *only* what happened in Palestine two thousand years ago, it wasn't just the local and temporal and personal, it's the other kingdom, it's the courts of God' (pp. 199–200). She urges him not to worry about first-century Judaism or the Church's history over many centuries, because 'it's mostly irrelevant to what matters' (p. 200).

A few pages later, Laurie journeys to the Sea of Galilee and finds this place, away from the 'tourists . . . and fake holy places', to be beautiful and refreshing. She stays there for several days, 'stumbling about the ruins . . . and going out with the fishermen in their boats while they cast their nets' (p. 204). Influenced by this ambience and reflecting on the places she has seen, Laurie feels moved to approach David's question from the opposite point of view. This corrective step in her presentation of Christianity is significant because her first response came close to translating the tradition's distinctive historical claims into timeless truths without remainder, risking the reduction or elimination of key elements of the particular story in order to make the religion more broadly appealing and relevant.[22] Balance is restored when she says: 'In all these places that I go through, I thought, he [Jesus] once was, he once taught and talked, and drew people after him like a magnet, as he is now drawing me' (p. 205). Laurie realizes that if David were present now and wanted to know how a first-century Jew and extravagant claims to universal truth could possibly be related, she would answer him differently: 'for by the sea of Galilee Christianity seemed local and temporal and personal after all, though it included Hagia Sophia and all the humanities and Oriens, *sol justitiae*, that has lighted every man who has come into the world' (p. 205).

Thus does Laurie deal with the scandal of particularity. The landscape of Palestine engages her associative powers. Here her imagination has room to play and to see connections, not only between finite and infinite, temporal and eternal, but also between her own little world and this larger cosmos of meaning. Her tentative apprehension of a deeper reality – an incipient awareness made possible by her insight into the relation of concrete (the facts of one man's life) and universal (ultimate reality) – has implications for her as well. Laurie's imaginative breakthrough not only helps her to understand realities outside her; it also threatens to impose a new order on her free and casual life. A sense of an ending may bring narrative coherence to a person's life-story, but an ending may be the last thing he or she wants to consider in the present moment: lines coming together to form a net.

At this point in her journey Laurie is not willing to heed the call of this place or to let her imagination run away with her; she won't be caught in a larger web of meaning. She 'would have liked to spend a long time in Galilee', fishing, rowing, painting and swimming; but 'I had to leave it, and I did not think I should come back' (pp. 205–6). The place represents too great a threat to her present life: 'it was too subversive, it filled me with notions and feelings that were dangerous to my life' (p. 206). That is, Galilee with all of its associations was likely to cause her to question the true nature of her life with her married lover and to lead her back to a realization of what she was missing.

In the days following Vere's death, Laurie, stricken with grief and remorse, rejects what he rejected, giving up what he mockingly called her 'church obsession'. She turns her back on the Church and all that it stands for, 'knowing that God is leaving us alone for ever; we have lost God and gained hell' (p. 276).

And yet, as Rose Macaulay delighted to point out, *The Towers of Trebizond* helped to convince not a few readers to turn *toward* the Church and what it stands for. Her novel had, she said, decided a young woman at a crucial moment in her life for the right course, and clergy read parts of it to ordinands besieged by doubt, without plunging them into deeper anguish. People saw it as a Christian book despite its conclusion.

Why? Not because its author said that her heroine would eventually re-enter the Church but rather because internal evidence suggests the following: the novel's ending is a fair rendering of grief and despair, but this level of intense grief (with attendant emotions) may not be permanent. Sufficient signs exist throughout the story to lend credibility to the supposition that the last pages of the novel do not represent the narrator's final thoughts on the subject of religious commitment. The Church, she says, 'has produced saints and martyrs and kindness and goodness, though these have also occurred freely outside it, and it is a wonderful and most extraordinary pageant of contradictions, and I, at least, want to be inside it, though it is foolishness to most of my friends' (p. 197).

Perhaps the best reason for believing that Laurie will not rest secure in her alienation is not so much the content of some of her statements as the form of her thinking throughout the novel. She is not only youthful and intelligent; she is also prone to exercising a flexible, indeed a persistently dialectical, imagination, one that is habitually given to considering subjects in pairs of things that are in tension with one another: the Church as life-giving/death-dealing, the Bible as accurate/misleading, Christ as individual/universal, the Christian faith as culturally embedded narrative/eternal wisdom, the Christian way as accessible/inaccessible. And in each of these pairs the virgule signifies the honest ambiguity of the relation: 'and' or 'or'?

Of course, deploying this argument to support the claim that Laurie will not always believe that she must stand outside the shimmering towers compels the complementary acknowledgment that, if she does rejoin the Church, she will not remain completely secure in her faith either. But the concerned reader can contemplate this outcome with equanimity. For Laurie, Christian fundamentalism or an infallible Church would be a problem – though one that she does not have to worry about, for, as she says, 'Anglicans have less certainty but more scope, and can use their imaginations more' (p. 203). Her imagination yields up images of a Church that, while weakened by modernity, is still sufficiently strong and capacious to accommodate her and others like her, carrying them along in their weakness and ignorance.

The Anglican Church, she remarks, 'seems to be playing some tremendous symphony; the music drifts singing about the arches and vaults, only faintly and partly apprehended by us, the ignorant armies that clash by night in perpetual assault and rout' – the final phrase, of course, borrowed in homage to 'Dover Beach', Matthew Arnold's famous poem about the erosion of religious faith (p. 234).

Faith and doubt in the life of Rose Macaulay

Readers of *The Towers of Trebizond* have often wondered whether Laurie speaks for Rose Macaulay. On a surface level at least, their voices are different. Laurie's prose style resembles that of a plucky and fairly glib young woman recounting her adventures in a letter to a trusted friend. Her writing typically consists of long sentences whose tumbling clauses are linked with conjunctions, one thought leading to the next and the next. Macaulay recalled that she had given Laurie a 'rather goofy, rambling prose style, to put the story at one remove from myself'.[23]

But the author would not have felt that she needed to 'put the story at one remove' if she had not written a novel that is so significantly autobiographical. 'The moral frame of the book', one critic has observed, 'is Laurie's fictional confession and, doubling it, the confessional testimony of the writer . . .'[24] As a result, at least two narrative voices are discernible in *Trebizond*, and, like a knot that contains one loop within a larger loop, two overlapping stories are present as well. Admittedly, in the case of this semi-autobiographical novel, following D. H. Lawrence's advice to 'trust the tale' is made more difficult by the fact that the artist and the tale are so intimately connected.

At the end of the last section of the present essay, for example, we heard Laurie speaking of the Church 'playing some tremendous symphony'. In a letter that Macaulay wrote to Father Hamilton Johnson in 1952, she spoke of the experience of 'being *in* the Church' as 'a wonderful corporate feeling of being carried along, being part of the body'. There are, she said, 'bits one doesn't yet grasp', but 'that doesn't matter to the whole pattern and movement in which one is involved', which is like 'a great sweeping symphony that one can hear a little of the meaning of now and then'.[25] In *The Towers of Trebizond*, three voices blend together: those of Laurie, of Rose Macaulay past, and of Rose Macaulay present.

The catalyst of the confession that made this story possible was the person to whom Macaulay wrote the letter just quoted: an Anglo-Catholic monk whom she had known when she was a young woman in London and with whom she had later lost touch. The Reverend Hamilton Johnson was a member of the Society of St John the Evangelist, the Cowley Fathers. After going through a stretch of spiritual questioning as an adolescent, Rose grew into a young woman with a serious religious bent. Like Laurie, she often said that Christianity was in her blood, as she had many clerical forebears on both sides of her family; but more than family tradition or custom was at work in her spiritual devotion. Particularly after attending a retreat at St Alban's, a High Church parish in Holborn, around 1909, Macaulay undertook the disciplined practice of her faith, regularly going to confession at St Edward's House in Westminster, which was the London headquarters of the Cowley Fathers. Whenever her usual priest was unable to hear her confession, Hamilton Johnson filled in for him. This acquaintance lasted for a little more than two years, until the autumn of 1916, when Father Johnson was transferred to the Cowley Fathers' community in Boston, Massachusetts.[26]

Two years later, in 1918, Rose Macaulay met the former Roman Catholic priest who would become her lover. Gerald O'Donovan, age 45, was the married father of three children. A minor novelist, at the end of the war he was in charge of the Italian section of the British government's propaganda department. Temporarily employed in the civil service, Macaulay, then 36, met O'Donovan when she was transferred to his department because of her fluency in Italian.[27] They fell in love and eventually began a long affair, which lasted until O'Donovan's death in 1942.

By 1922 Macaulay felt that she could no longer make her confession to a priest or receive the bread and wine at celebrations of Holy Communion; thus began a separation from the Church which was to last for nearly 30 years.[28] During this time, she continued to feel 'Anglican', as she put it, but she was 'an Anglo-agnostic', for whom Anglicanism had dwindled down to 'a matter of taste and affection . . . rather than of belief'.[29]

This long period of estrangement began to come to an end on 29 August 1950, when Macaulay quite out of the blue received a letter from her former interim confessor, Father Hamilton Johnson.[30] He wanted her to know how much he had enjoyed her historical novel,

They Were Defeated.[31] Although they were never again to meet face to face, these two cousins – for they eventually discovered that they were fourth cousins – enjoyed a strong epistolary friendship that was to last until Rose's death in 1958.

On 12 January 1951, less than five months after receiving this clergyman's fan letter, Macaulay went to St Edward's House and made her confession to a priest.[32] Two days later, she wrote to thank Father Johnson, from whom she had already received, in her words, *'absolutiones transmarinae'*. These absolutions from across the ocean were not, she told him, *'nothae* [illegitimate] . . . whatever church law may say'.[33]

In her seventieth year Rose Macaulay returned to the Church of England as a communicant. She adopted a rule of life, and each morning she attended the early celebration at Grosvenor Chapel, in South Audley Street, not far from her London flat. Small and austerely beautiful, Grosvenor was a chapel of ease built of brick in 1730. By the end of the First World War, it had evolved into a liberal Anglo-Catholic church that featured dignified services – high but not extreme – which suited Macaulay's religious sensibilities.[34] 'On the whole, what makes Grosvenor Chapel perfect . . . is that people never bother you there,' commented the poet John Betjeman, a close friend of both Rose Macaulay and Austin Farrer. 'The whole point of it is that you aren't asked to join something.'[35] On Sundays Macaulay often attended St Paul's Church, Knightsbridge, which, as a large suburban parish, provided a different but equally agreeable sort of religious experience. Over time she came to love the Anglican tradition more and more, and she felt her universe expanding.[36]

It expanded to make room for, among other things, contrition. She confessed to Father Johnson that 'long years of wrong-doing build a kind of blank – or nearly blank – wall between oneself and God', a wall constructed not by God but by 'one's own actions and rejections'.[37] Her love affair, she told him, was too costly an endeavour, both to the lovers themselves and to the others involved. 'I didn't know that before, but I do now . . . If only I had refused, and gone on refusing. It's not a question of forgiveness, but of irrevocable damage done.' Like Laurie, she knew what it was to choose between her lover and God. 'I see now why belief in God fades away and has to go, while one is leading a life one knows to be wrong. The two can't live together. It doesn't give even intellectual acceptance its chance. Now it *has* its chance.' She still did not 'attach much importance to *details* of belief . . . But I hold on to your remark – "we may be sure that at the bottom of the whole business there is a personal relationship", which is possibly all that matters. After what has occurred to me lately, I *know* there is.'[38]

Rose Macaulay's universe also expanded to give her a new quality of existence, reflected in her day-to-day interactions. Her biographer Constance Babington Smith, who knew her, said: 'The tenor of her secret, inner life, long one of despairing pessimism, was . . . gradually transformed into one of serenity and hope.'[39] Her sister Jean remarked upon a change for the better in Rose's character: 'After her "conversion" Rose became gentler, softer, and she didn't say such spiteful things any more.'[40] And when he reviewed the first published volume of her letters to Father Johnson, Harold Nicolson said of his friend: 'Her joyous faith halved half her worries and doubled all her joys.'[41]

Rose Macaulay believed that human beings are interesting because each person is a mess of contradictions.[42] Certainly both she and her creation, Laurie, are complicated beings. The post-1950 Macaulay appears to represent the full, committed life of faith that follows on the stage that Austin Farrer called initial faith. This vantage point afforded her a perspective on her life which enabled her to see and to depict with feeling and accuracy Laurie's hard struggle with Christianity. 'I, too, you know, felt Laurie's half-stunned insensibility, and even aversion, towards the Church for some time after the man I had loved for so long died,' she told Father Johnson. 'I don't take Laurie far enough in her life to get to where she, as I did, encounters some influence that brings her church-ward. But of course it came: feeling as she always had about the Church and about separation from God, she would not for very long be outside it.'[43]

Just as we saw in the case of Laurie, however, that a neatly diachronic developmental scheme failed to reckon squarely with the complexity of her position, so in the case of the author do we find contrarieties contained within one character. Laurie's situation called on us to descry faith alongside doubt and defiance; Macaulay's calls for acknowledgment of doubt alongside faith. For this reason we can properly think of three, not merely two, voices in *Trebizond*. Besides being her own unique fictional self, the questing and questioning

Laurie stands both for the Rose Macaulay of the troubled past and for the post-conversion Rose.

Like Augustine, Macaulay knew that the strand of certainty is an elusive beach; its shifting sands mean that Christian conversion is never complete and final. Toward the end of her life, she told her sister Jean that 'religious belief is too uncertain and shifting a ground (with me) to speak of lying or truth in connection with it. One believes in patches, and it ["believe"] is a vague, inaccurate word. I could never say "I believe in God" in the same sense that I could say "I believe in the sun & moon & stars".'[44]

As Augustine makes clear in the *Confessions*, his conversion did not mean that he had now arrived safely in port; the harbour of the convert is regularly buffeted by storms. In another image, even the baptized Christian must remain an invalid. Augustine's biographer Peter Brown writes that the Bishop of Hippo was like the injured man whom the Good Samaritan found by the side of the road. Augustine knew that he had been saved, but he also knew that 'he must be content to endure, for the rest of his life, a prolonged and precarious convalescence in the "Inn" of the Church'.[45]

This understanding of faith helps to account for Rose Macaulay's loyalty to Anglo-Catholicism. The Protestant emphasis on the situation of the individual believer in relation to God seemed too narrowly focused to fit her life. 'One wants to get the right balance', she said, 'between Protestantism (the individual seeking after God) and Catholicism (the seeking through the Church), neglecting neither.'[46] She favoured a church that was like a 'tremendous symphony', even when – especially when – she felt religiously unmusical and even though there were parts of the score that she could never get hold of. It helped her to know that she was a member of a larger body – to have, as she put it, the 'wonderful corporate feeling of being carried along'.[47]

Her personal faith was not enough to sustain her. For Rose Macaulay, trying to be 'spiritual' without also being 'religious' would have meant impoverishment and the death of the spirit, not its liberation. She knew that she needed the Eucharist, confession and absolution, the guidance and encouragement provided by sound preaching, the discipline of prayer and the fellowship of other Christians.[48]

Bethlehem, the Virgin Birth, the bodily resurrection of Christ: these were among the important stories and tenets of the Christian faith which gave her pause.[49] 'I would almost *rather* think', she told Father Johnson, that Christ 'was born like us and died like us, and that it was His spirit only that lived after death, taking the form His friends would recognize . . . I felt, at the Easter mass, that here was Christ risen and with us, and I didn't care how.'[50] She questioned whether the Apostle Paul believed in the empty tomb.[51] And she could not help thinking that churches placed too much weight on the doctrine of the Atonement. For this reason she was not fond of Passion Week – it was 'not my favourite season' – for 'the Church seems always to have clung to its ancient sacrificial Hebrew notions, which haunt its interpretation of Good Friday'.[52]

In addition, Macaulay had no use for a literal understanding of the Fall of Adam. She was not at all certain what happens to the faithful departed: 'Oh what happens to the dead? *Lux perpetua*, we pray; but in what mode, and what individual consciousness do they have of us? We can't know.'[53] And she could not go along with those who hopefully awaited the Second Coming of Christ:

> Now we have Bp Wand [of London] who looks for the Second Coming any minute, which must make life exciting for him. I expect he hopes for it before his death, which would save him a lot of bother about his will, tidying up etc. I should like this too, but have no hopes for it . . . He sounded as if he had no doubts about it. I wonder how many people think this.[54]

Rose Macaulay's customary position was not unlike Laurie's: no one could possibly see the complete picture. 'All [that is needed]', she told Father Johnson, 'is a grain of wholesome scepticism about having the whole truth; a thing . . . which is needed by both Christians and secularists . . .'[55] Non-believers as well as Christians, she asserted, ought to strive for intellectual humility in the face of mystery. In her book *Personal Pleasures* (1936), written during her period of estrangement from Christianity, Macaulay included brief essays on both 'believing' and 'disbelieving'. In the latter she wrote that 'I must beware . . . of too wide and too deep an incredulity, and remember that there are many things yet hid from us, and that really everything is extremely peculiar.'[56]

'But,' she asked Father Johnson, 'if my mind can't quite take certain things – such as the physical Resurrection – does it matter so long as it doesn't get in the way of belief in Christ as master and saviour and helper, to be sought and served?' He urged her to yield to God the mind that was hers, not an ideal mind that she did not possess. In reply, she acknowledged that 'God takes [our minds] and does what he can with them. And of course in time they might develop new powers of faith . . .'[57]

Rose Macaulay's brand of Anglicanism was – to use the quasi-technical terms of this tradition – high and broad: that is, liturgically catholic and intellectually engaged.[58] She praised the Cambridge Platonists, the seventeenth-century divines who spoke of the indwelling of God in the mind and advocated tolerance and comprehension in the Church: 'I love those Cambridge 17th century men . . . and their stress on the light that lighteth every man and the Deiform seed in the soul . . .'[59] In her philosophy of the Christian life, she was very much a latter-day Cambridge Platonist: 'what I believe in', Rose told her sister Jean, '[is] the Light that lights every man, trained up by reason.' The Bible and the Church, she said, are 'only products of the Light, not its sources'.[60]

In her personal devotions she often used the Great Antiphons, which we heard Laurie quote to David. 'Please sometimes say . . . "*O Sapientia*" [for me],' Macaulay urged Father Johnson. 'And "*O Oriens*". Light and wisdom. With those one can't go far wrong.'[61] She treasured these Advent invocations and knew *O Oriens* by heart.[62] An English translation of this Latin prayer is 'O Dawn of the East, brightness of the light eternal, and Sun of Justice, come and enlighten them that sit in darkness and in the shadow of death.' For herself and for others, Macaulay prayed for and looked forward to the arrival of this illumination of heart and mind.[63] Not the mind only but the conscience and the will also: Macaulay's approach to the religious life valued the Christian idea of 'bringing . . . our wills into harmony with Christ'.[64]

Conclusion

Laurie, the main character in *The Towers of Trebizond*, is a person of fortitude. She will endure, but whether she will prevail depends upon the development of her imagination. Like her human creator, she possesses an imagination for evil. She has learned – the hard way – to identify the causes and effects of evil in the cellarage of her own psyche and in the lives of others. What she lacks is an imagination for forgiveness and healing – or someone to bring to life the potentiality within the imagination that is already hers.

For that plot development, however, we need to turn to two other narratives associated with Rose Macaulay: first, the biography of the author herself. Her story reveals the importance of patience as an essential virtue for all those seeking to live the life of faith. Rose Macaulay's journey was a long one, full of hazards and detours. And, like Augustine, even when she had 'arrived', she could not rest completely easy, confident that she now had all the answers. Rowan Williams, the 104th Archbishop of Canterbury, stresses the key role that patience plays in the outlook and practice of faithful Christians. Believers 'do not expect human words to solve their problems rapidly', he observes; 'they do not expect the Bible to yield up its treasures overnight, [and] they do not look for the triumphant march of an ecclesiastical institution'. Instead, they know 'they live among immensities of meaning'; they 'live in the wake of a divine action which defies summary explanation'. Therefore Christians properly 'take it for granted that [they are] always learning, moving in and out of speech and silence'.[65]

The second narrative of forgiveness and healing is Rose Macaulay's other great novel, *The World My Wilderness* (1950), a story vitally concerned with the effects of the Second World War on civilization and particularly on the lives of children. This novel has a protagonist, 17-year-old Barbary, whose imagination has been corrupted by violence and fear. Sullen, suspicious and defiant, Barbary is, as one literary scholar has observed, 'thoroughly lost, thoroughly pathetic, and very much worth saving'.[66]

In France during the Occupation, as a member of a band of boys and girls assisting the Maquis, Barbary was brutally and far too rapidly transformed from a child of innocence into a child of experience. After the war, living in London, she continues to think that she must ever be on guard against the enemy. Still provisioned with images of Gestapo and 'collabos', of death and betrayal, her imagination now misleads her. It fails to link her to reality, to life and love; instead it pulls her toward destruction. Morally adrift, she has only one religious belief – 'in hell'.[67] She rejects both country house and town house, preferring to live amid 'the ruined waste lands . . . the broken walls and foundations . . . the roofless, gaping churches, the stone flights of stairs climbing high into emptiness'.[68] The bombed-out ruins of the City are, she believes, where she belongs: 'at the waste margins of civilization . . . where other outcasts lurked, and questions were not asked'.[69]

Until liberated by understanding, forgiveness and reconciliation, Barbary's imagination is an example of a human faculty gone tragically awry, showing how the imagination can distort reality and mislead a person rather than enlighten.[70] In addition, her story demonstrates the immature imagination's vulnerability to the shaping influences of adults. *The World My Wilderness* is Macaulay's take on the lasting significance of the narratives that we tell our children – or, more accurately, that our children hear from us, whether we want them to or not. From these narratives children learn their own individual stories. The images children ingest will provision their imaginations and inform their characters for years to come, for each person's imagination is far less an individual achievement than a family endeavour and a community enterprise.

Notes

1 Rose Macaulay to Jean Macaulay, 24 July 1958, in Rose Macaulay, *Letters to a Sister*, ed. Constance Babington Smith (New York: Atheneum, 1964), p. 281.

2 Quoted in Constance Babington Smith, *Rose Macaulay* (London: Collins, 1972), p. 204.

3 Rose Macaulay to Jean Macaulay, 24 July 1958, in Macaulay, *Letters to a Sister*, p. 281.

4 Gloria G. Fromm, 'The Worldly and Unworldly Fortunes of Rose Macaulay', *The New Criterion* 5, no. 2 (October 1986), p. 44.

5 Rose Macaulay to Revd J. C. Hamilton Johnson, SSJE, 14 November 1956, in Rose Macaulay, *Last Letters to a Friend, 1952–1958*, ed. Constance Babington Smith (New York: Atheneum, 1963), p. 239.

6 C. S. Lewis, *Letters to Malcolm: Chiefly on Prayer* (New York: Harcourt, Brace & World, 1963), p. 10.

7 Rose Macaulay to Revd J. C. Hamilton Johnson, 1 June 1951, in Rose Macaulay, *Letters to a Friend, 1950–1952*, ed. Constance Babington Smith (New York: Atheneum, 1962), pp. 232–3.

8 Barbara Reynolds, 'Take Away the Camel, and All is Revealed', *Church Times*, no. 7177 (8 September 2000), pp. 14–15.

9 Judith Moore, 'Rose Macaulay: A Model for Christian Feminists', *Christian Century* 95, no. 37 (15 November 1978), p. 1101.

10 Philip Sidney, *Sir Philip Sidney's Defense of Poesy*, ed. Lewis Soens (Lincoln: University of Nebraska Press, 1970), p. 17.

11 See Donald T. Williams, 'Christian Poetics, Past and Present', in *The Christian Imagination*, ed. Leland Ryken (Colorado Springs: Shaw Books, 2002), pp. 9–11.

12 Rose Macaulay, *The Towers of Trebizond* (1956; repr., New York: New York Review Books, 2003), p. 10. Hereafter cited within the text.

13 Rose Macaulay to Revd J. C. Hamilton Johnson, 6 February 1956, in Macaulay, *Last Letters to a Friend*, p. 219.

14 Rose Macaulay to Revd J. C. Hamilton Johnson, 14 November 1956, in Macaulay, *Last Letters to a Friend*, p. 239.

15 D. H. Lawrence, *Studies in Classic American Literature* (1923; repr., New York: Viking, 1961), p. 2.

16 Alice Crawford, *Paradise Pursued: The Novels of Rose Macaulay* (Madison: Fairleigh Dickinson University Press, 1995), p. 155.

17 Jean Macaulay to Constance Babington Smith, 7 November 1961, Papers of Rose Macaulay, Trinity College, Cambridge University, quoted in Crawford, *Paradise Pursued*, p. 154.

18 Crawford, *Paradise Pursued*, p. 155.

19 Austin Farrer, *Saving Belief: A Discussion of Essentials* (1964; repr., Harrisburg, PA: Morehouse, 1994), p. 21.

20 Farrer, *Saving Belief*, pp. 6–9.

21 Rowan A. Greer, *Broken Lights and Mended Lives* (University Park: Pennsylvania State University Press, 1986).

22 David Brown, *Tradition and Imagination: Revelation and Change* (Oxford: Oxford University Press, 2004), pp. 368–70.

23 Rose Macaulay, quoted in Alice R. Bensen, *Rose Macaulay* (New York: Twayne, 1969), p. 158.

24 Bensen, *Rose Macaulay*, p. 157.

25 Rose Macaulay to Revd J. C. Hamilton Johnson, 14 June 1952, in Macaulay, *Letters to a Friend*, p. 325.

26 Constance Babington Smith, introduction to Macaulay, *Letters to a Friend*, pp. 13–17.

27 Fromm, 'Worldly and Unworldly Fortunes', p. 40.

28 Crawford, *Paradise Pursued*, p. 18.

29 Rose Macaulay to Revd J. C. Hamilton Johnson, 9 February 1951, in Macaulay, *Letters to a Friend*, p. 69.

30 Jane Emery, *Rose Macaulay: A Writer's Life* (London: John Murray, 1991), p. 298.

31 Crawford, *Paradise Pursued*, p. 146.

32 Emery, *Rose Macaulay*, p. 301.

33 Rose Macaulay to Revd J. C. Hamilton Johnson, 14 January 1951, in Macaulay, *Letters to a Friend*, p. 54.

34 Emery, *Rose Macaulay*, pp. 303–4.

35 John Betjeman, introduction to *Godly Mayfair*, ed. Ann Callender (London: Grosvenor Chapel, 1980), pp. iv–v.

36 Emery, *Rose Macaulay*, p. 305.

37 Rose Macaulay to Revd J. C. Hamilton Johnson, 15 December 1950, in Macaulay, *Letters to a Friend*, p. 39.

38 Rose Macaulay to Revd J. C. Hamilton Johnson, 28 January 1951, in Macaulay, *Letters to a Friend*, p. 62.

39 Babington Smith, *Rose Macaulay*, p. 192.

40 Quoted in Babington Smith, *Rose Macaulay*, p. 200.

41 Quoted in Babington Smith, *Rose Macaulay*, p. 213.

42 Emery, *Rose Macaulay*, p. 297.

43 Rose Macaulay to Revd J. C. Hamilton Johnson, 1 October 1956, in Macaulay, *Last Letters to a Friend*, p. 233.

44 Rose Macaulay to Jean Macaulay, 24 July 1958, in Macaulay, *Letters to a Sister*, p. 282.

45 Peter Brown, *Augustine of Hippo: A Biography* (Berkeley: University of California Press, 1967), p. 365.

46 Rose Macaulay to Revd J. C. Hamilton Johnson, 11 July 1952, in Macaulay, *Letters to a Friend*, p. 338.

47 Rose Macaulay to Revd J. C. Hamilton Johnson, 14 June 1952, in Macaulay, *Letters to a Friend*, p. 325.

48 Emery, *Rose Macaulay*, p. 303.

49 Emery, *Rose Macaulay*, p. 302.

50 Rose Macaulay to Revd J. C. Hamilton Johnson, 27 March 1951, in Macaulay, *Letters to a Friend*, p. 107.

51 Rose Macaulay to Revd J. C. Hamilton Johnson, 8 April 1951, in Macaulay, *Letters to a Friend*, p. 110.

52 Rose Macaulay to Revd J. C. Hamilton Johnson, 6 April 1954, in Macaulay, *Last Letters to a Friend*, p. 152.

53 Rose Macaulay to Revd J. C. Hamilton Johnson, 22 August 1952, in Macaulay, *Letters to a Friend*, p. 352.

54 Rose Macaulay to Jean Macaulay, 4 December 1956, in Macaulay, *Letters to a Sister*, p. 208.

55 Rose Macaulay to Revd J. C. Hamilton Johnson, 11 February 1952, in Macaulay, *Letters to a Friend*, p. 267.

56 Rose Macaulay, *Personal Pleasures* (New York: Macmillan, 1936), p. 159.

57 Rose Macaulay to Revd J. C. Hamilton Johnson, 15 February 1951, in Macaulay, *Letters to a Friend*, p. 74.

58 Constance Babington Smith, introduction to Macaulay, *Last Letters to a Friend*, p. 22.

59 Rose Macaulay to Revd J. C. Hamilton Johnson, 6 April 1954, in Macaulay, *Last Letters to a Friend*, p. 152.
60 Rose Macaulay to Jean Macaulay, 19 March 1953, in Macaulay, *Letters to a Sister*, p. 151.
61 Rose Macaulay to Revd J. C. Hamilton Johnson, 11 February 1952, in Macaulay, *Letters to a Friend*, p. 267.
62 Rose Macaulay to Revd J. C. Hamilton Johnson, 2 January 1952, in Macaulay, *Letters to a Friend*, pp. 245–6.
63 Babington Smith, introduction to Macaulay, *Last Letters to a Friend*, pp. 19–20.
64 Rose Macaulay to Revd J. C. Hamilton Johnson, 17 May 1953, in Macaulay, *Last Letters to a Friend*, p. 98.
65 Rowan Williams, *Anglican Identities* (Cambridge, MA: Cowley, 2003), p. 7.
66 Harvey Curtis Webster, *After the Trauma: Representative British Novelists since 1920* (Lexington: University Press of Kentucky, 1970), p. 27.
67 Rose Macaulay, *The World My Wilderness* (1950; repr., London: Virago, 1983), p. 174.
68 Macaulay, *The World My Wilderness*, p. 61.
69 Macaulay, *The World My Wilderness*, p. 110.
70 Brown, *Tradition and Imagination*, pp. 287–97.

Figure 6 J. R. R. Tolkien.
Pamela Chandler/Arenapal.

6

J. R. R. Tolkien: His sorrowful
vision of joy

RALPH C. WOOD

Among the chief accomplishments in our growing appreciation of Tolkien's *The Lord of the Rings* is the consensus view that it is indubitably a Christian epic. When he called it 'a fundamentally religious and Catholic work', Tolkien was not being merely pious; he was also stating the basic intention of his grand *Legendarium*, as he called it.[1] In the version collected by Christopher Tolkien, it runs to 12 volumes, and more items keep trickling forth. It is the huge collection of tales and languages, characters and events, genealogies and maps that Tolkien spent his entire adult life inventing, linking, rearranging, but never of course completing. How could he, since his aim was to retell, in mythic form, the entire story of the cosmos as Christians understand it? If Tolkien had enjoyed several more lives beyond his allotted 81 years, he might have extended his mythological project to include the Incarnation, crucifixion and resurrection – perhaps even providing a foretaste of life in the world to come.

Despite his overtly theological intention, Tolkien was no apologist. He sought, instead, to follow the example of the anonymous Christian author of *Beowulf* – namely, to imbue his work with a subtle and often silent Christian subtext; to make his 'message' (insofar as there could be any formulaic 'theme') lie far beneath the surface, so deeply sunk and yet so centrally constitutive that it would become evident only when one peered into its depths. Yet so many readers have discerned the joyful gospel undergirding Tolkien's epic that we run the risk of ignoring another and darker side of his work. I refer to the pervasive gloom characterizing the whole of his imaginative vision. Although Tolkien's sombreness is most evident in *The Silmarillion*, which contains a version of the *Húrin* story, it is also present in *The Lord of the Rings*.

The purpose of this essay, therefore, is to account for both the joy and the sorrow at work in Tolkien's massive *oeuvre*. To do so, we must first examine the redemptive character of the Ring epic, especially as it is focused on the unexpected heroism of Tolkien's diminutive and ostensibly weak creatures called hobbits, as they win their surprising victory over Sauron and the Ring of Power. We shall then, in the second section, look at one of his most disturbing works, *The Children of Húrin*, as an example of this perennial fascination with those things that are not free but fated. Only then will we be able, in a brief final section, to determine the right relation between doom and delight as they characterize Tolkien's vision.

The melancholy vision of *The Lord of the Rings*

The Lord of the Rings was not a self-consciously Christian work in the beginning, Tolkien confessed, but it increasingly became so during his many revisions of it. 'It is about God and His sole right to divine honour . . .'[2] Thus does justice stand at the centre of Tolkien's vision. Life within a cosmos that is the creator's utter gift should elicit proper praise and worship of God. As a thoroughgoing Augustinian, Tolkien held that our fundamental life-task is the setting of our desires and loves in right order, honouring God above all other things, and thus loving these other things according to their relatively subordinate worth. It is just such honour that the rebel *vala* named Melkor refused to grant Ilúvatar, the divine creator. In an act of proud rebellion akin to Lucifer's revolt against Yahweh, Melkor sought his own autonomy, living entirely for himself, thus ruining the cosmic harmony as Ilúvatar had orchestrated it. Before he was finally defeated, Melkor (renamed Morgoth = Dark Enemy) recruited a *maia* named Sauron ('the Abominable') to his cause.

Here we enter the actual setting of *The Lord of the Rings*, since it is Sauron the Dark Lord who has fashioned a single Ruling Ring by whose coercive power he schemes to dominate the then-known world called Middle-earth. Yet it is noteworthy that Ilúvatar has suborned neither Morgoth nor Sauron to his service, nor has he simply crushed their revolt in order to prevent their potential ruin of his cosmos. Such an act of omnipotent will would have been for Ilúvatar to perform an act of 'unmaking', reversing the very order of his good creation, which is based on free assent rather than absolute control. Such coercive force, by contrast, is Sauron's *modus operandi*. He is intent upon establishing his own supremacy over all things, and he reads all others by his own light. He believes that anyone, having once possessed the virtually absolute power afforded by the Ring, would be determined to use it – especially the magical power to make its wearer invisible. Though Sauron's craft and power are great, as his fashioning of the Ring demonstrates, he can fashion nothing good, but only parodies and mockeries of benevolent things. It is clear that Tolkien shares St Augustine's understanding of evil as *privatio boni*, the privation or absence of true being, the perversion or deformation of the good. Evil exists only parasitically, leeching off the good, having only the negative power to damage and destroy. Exactly because evil has no proper substance or essence, however, the Devil can feign numerous *appearances*, embodying himself in all sorts and conditions of deceit.

In the *Rings* epic, Sauron has taken the form of a terrible all-seeing Eye. He is a virtual Panopticon, able to discern the outward operation of all things, but opaque to the inward workings of motive and purpose. Sauron's fatal lack is not intelligence, therefore, but sympathy. He cannot 'feel with', and so he is incapable of community. He assumes that Frodo and his friends will seek to overthrow him and to establish their own sovereignty. Yet Sauron's calculus of self-interest blinds him to the surprising strategy of the Company. Under Gandalf's leadership, they decide not to hide, much less to use, the Ring, but to take it straight back to the Land of Mordor – Sauron's own lair – there to incinerate it in the volcanic cracks of Mount Doom.

Frodo proves to be a fit bearer of the Ring because he does not seek but only reluctantly accepts his task. Not only does he possess native powers of courage and resistance; he is also albeit unaccountably summoned. Early in the narrative, Frodo finds that an authentic Quest – unlike mere 'there and back again' adventures – is neither voluntary in nature nor assured in its outcome. Neither does it necessarily entail the search for or recovery of a great treasure, as happens when his Uncle Bilbo aids the dwarves in *The Hobbit*. On the contrary, Frodo is not called to find but to lose, indeed to destroy, the deadly Ring of total control. The epic's compelling interest lies largely in following the complex ways whereby Frodo remains both faithful and unfaithful to his calling until the very end. Because they are bound by the blessed ties of unsworn commitment to their singular task – drawn ever more closely together into a shared life of sacrifice – Frodo and his friends learn what for Tolkien is the deepest truth: how to surrender one's life to the good, how to 'lose' evil treasures, and thus how to live with moral and spiritual concentration, as Gandalf memorably declares: 'All we have to decide is what to do with the time that is given us.'[3]

For Tolkien, the chief question – and thus the real quest – concerns the proper means for 'redeeming the time'. The great temptation is to take short-cuts, to follow the easy way, to arrive quickly. In the antique world of Middle-earth, magic offers the surest escape from slowness and suffering. It is the equivalent of our machines. Both ancient and modern magic provide what Tolkien called *immediacy*: 'speed, reduction of labour, and reduction also to a minimum (or vanishing point) of the gap between the idea or desire and the result or effect'.[4] The magic of haste is the method chosen by those who are in a hurry, who lack patience, who cannot wait. Sauron wins converts because he provides his followers with the necromancy to achieve such instant results by coercing the wills of others, giving them brute strength to accomplish allegedly grand ends by cursory means.

The noble who refuse such haste prove, alas, to be most nobly tempted. Gandalf, the Christ-like wizard who literally lays down his life for his friends, knows that he is an unworthy bearer of the Ring – not because he has evil designs that he wants secretly to accomplish, but rather because his desire to do good is so great. Gandalf's native pity, when combined with the omnipotent strength of the Ring, would transform him into an all-forgiving, justice-denying magus, not a true wizard filled with the wisdom indicated in his title, for the Anglo-Saxon word *wys* means wise. Lady Galadriel, the elven queen, also refuses the Ring of coercion. It would make her enormous beauty mesmerizing. Those who had freely admired her loveliness would have no choice but to worship her slavishly. Rare among modern writers, Tolkien understood that evil's subtlest semblance is not with the ugly but with the gorgeous. 'I shall not be dark,' Galadriel warns, 'but beautiful and terrible as the Morning and the Night! Fair as the Sea and the Sun and the Snow upon the Mountain! Dreadful as the Storm and the Lightning! Stronger than the foundations of the earth. All shall love me and despair!'[5]

The hobbits are worthy opponents of the allurement of the Ring exactly because their life-aims are so very modest. Wanting nothing more than to preserve the freedom of their own peaceable Shire, they have no grandiose ambitions. Their meekness uniquely qualifies them to destroy the Ring in the Cracks of Doom. Theirs is a Quest that can be accomplished by the small even more aptly than by the great – by ordinary folks far more than by conventional heroes. In fact, the figure who gradually emerges as the rightful successor to Frodo is the least likely hobbit of them all, the comically inept, grammar-slaughtering, xenophobic – but also name-fulfilling – creature, Samwise Gamgee.

Precisely in the unlikely heroism of the small but doughty does Tolkien's pre-Christian world become most Christian and joyful. Whether in the ancient Nordic and Germanic, or else in the Greek and Roman worlds, only the strong and extraordinary are capable of heroism. The great man stands apart from his mediocre kith. He outdistances them in every way, whether in courage or in knowledge. It is not so in Middle-earth. The greatness of the Nine Walkers lies in the modesty of both their abilities and their accomplishments. Their strength lies in their weakness, in their solidarity as a company unwilling to wield controlling power over others. It turns them into literal *com-panis*: those who break bread together. Though the Fellowship contains representatives from all of the Free Peoples, some of them have been historic enemies – especially the dwarves and the elves. Yet no shallow notion of diversity binds them together. They are united not only by their common hatred of evil, but also by their ever-increasing, ever more self-surrendering love for each other. Through their long communal struggle, they learn that there is a power greater than mere might. It springs not chiefly from the forswearing of force, but from minds and hearts united in a high and holy calling.

The animating power of this Company is the much-maligned virtue called pity. It is a word that has come to have malodorous connotations, as if it entailed a certain condescension toward its recipients – as if the one who grants pity stands above them in moral and spiritual superiority. Knowing well that pity was the quality that Nietzsche most despised in Christianity, but also that the word derives from the antique Roman elevation of *pietas* as a fundamental reverence toward everything to which we owe our lives, Tolkien transforms the term into the epic's chief virtue. Frodo has learned the meaning of pity from his Uncle Bilbo. When he first obtained the Ring from the vile creature called Gollum, Bilbo had the chance to kill him but did not. Frodo is perplexed by this refusal. 'Tis a pity, he contends, that Bilbo did not slay such an evil one. This phrase angers the wise Gandalf. It prompts him to make the single most important declaration in the entire Ring epic:

> 'Pity? It was pity that stayed his hand. Pity, and Mercy: not to strike without need. And he has been well rewarded, Frodo. Be sure that [Bilbo] took so little hurt from the evil, and escaped in the end, because he began his ownership of the Ring so. With Pity.'
>
> 'I am sorry,' said Frodo. 'But . . . I do not feel any pity for Gollum. . . . He deserves death.'
>
> 'Deserves it! I daresay he does [replies Gandalf]. Many that live deserve death. And some that die deserve life. Can you give it to them? Then do not be too eager to deal out death in judgement. . . . the pity of Bilbo will rule the fate of many – yours not least.'[6]

Gandalf the pre-Christian wizard here announces the unstrained quality of Christian mercy that is completely unknown to the pagan world. Not to grant the wicked their just penalty is, for the ancient Greeks, to commit an even greater injustice. As a creature far more sinning than sinned against, Gollum thus *deserves* his misery. He has committed Cain's crime of fratricide in acquiring the Ring. Even so, Gandalf insists on pity, despite Frodo's protest that Gollum be given justice. If all died who warrant punishment, none would live, answers Gandalf. Many perish who have earned life, Gandalf declares, and yet who can restore them? Neither hobbits nor humans can live by the stones of merit alone. Hence Gandalf's call for pity and patience: the willingness to forgive trespasses and to wait on slow-working providence rather than rushing to self-righteous judgment. 'The pity of Bilbo will rule the fate of many' gradually becomes the motto of Tolkien's epic, as the phrase appears like a leitmotiv in all three volumes.

In fact, it is pity that produces, though seemingly by inadvertence, the final victory over Sauron. In what is surely the most surprising turn in the entire narrative, Frodo refuses at the end to surrender the dread band of omnipotence suspended from his neck. Frodo is deceived by his own successes – his repeated refusals to wield its triple powers of coercion and invisibility and longevity. He has persevered to the end, it seems, and thus readied himself for his final act: the destruction of Sauron's Ruling Ring. Yet these victories have, ironically, put him ever more fully under the power of the Ring, as he confesses to Sam. Despite his exceeding weakness of bodily strength – so wasted by hunger and suffering that Sam has to carry him up the mountain – he speaks with a power and force that the frightened Sam has never heard before. It's clear that his master's freedom of will has been virtually overwhelmed by Sauron, causing him not finally to fulfill but utterly to repudiate his mission. Rather than flinging the Ring into the melting magma, Frodo verily shouts his defiance: 'I have come,' he said. 'But I do not choose now to do what I came to do. I will not do this deed. The Ring is mine!'[7]

Frodo's words in an earlier version of the text were somewhat different: 'I have come to the end. But I cannot do what I came to do. I will not do it.'[8] Tolkien feared, however, that his original phrasing, especially the word 'cannot', might seem to exonerate Frodo, as if he had failed from sheer exhaustion rather than at least partial disobedience. Frodo's free consent to the Ring's seductive strength serves at the same time to demonstrate its power over him, as the Ring becomes a virtual ventriloquist who has made Frodo its mouthpiece. Tolkien thus reveals the dark paradox that our freedom can seem to be totally overwhelmed by external forces and yet remain at least minimally free. Frodo is thus a responsible agent, and not a pure victim.

Only because Frodo had earlier insisted on forgiving Gollum, and only because the ordinarily suspicious Sam spares him again in the end, is the wretched creature still present. He has trailed them all the way to the fissure of the volcanic mountain. It is not Frodo who destroys the Ring, by way of supreme faithfulness to his high calling, as we hoped and as Tolkien has led us to expect. Much to our surprise and disappointment, Frodo fails. It is the greedy Gollum who bites the Ring from Frodo's finger and, while dancing his jig of joy, tumbles backward into the inferno, dissolving the Ring with him.

There is hardly a more sombre dereliction in the whole of Anglophone literature. As C. S. Lewis rightly noted, a 'profound melancholy' pervades the entire epic. Despite Tolkien's claim to have imbued his epic with profound Christian convictions, even if silently, his great work climaxes with a grand victory won only through a woeful defeat. The conundrum that Tolkien's readers and critics have not thus far resolved is precisely this: why such a melancholy ending? The question is compounded by Tolkien's celebrated argument, made in his splendid essay 'On Fairy-Stories', that when fantasy reaches its fullest achievement, it strikes deeper truth than other literary forms – not in spite but precisely *because* of its happy endings.

True fantasies finish happily, Tolkien argues, thus providing consolation for life's tragedy and sorrow. Yet their felicitous outcome is not escapist. The ultimate victory is always produced by a disaster, by a sudden and cataclysmic turn of events, which issues in surprising deliverance. Tolkien invents a word to describe this saving cataclysm. He calls it a *eucatastrophe*: a happy calamity that does not deny the awful reality of *dyscatastrophe* – of human wreck and ruin. The miraculous though violent turnabout serves to demonstrate that death and defeat are not final; instead, the ultimate truth is Joy – 'Joy beyond the walls of the world, poignant as grief'.⁹ For Tolkien, the resurrection is the ultimately eucatastrophic event, for the world's salvation is won in and through the worst of evils, the crucifixion. Hence the link between fairy-story and gospel: 'this story is supreme; and it is true. Art has been verified. God is the Lord, of angels, and of men – and of elves. Legend and History have met and fused.'¹⁰

Yet where, if at all, is there any eucatastrophe to be found in *The Lord of the Rings*? Certainly not in the final scenes. They are among Tolkien's most melancholy pages. Although the Ring is destroyed, the victory is won in spite of the hero. Frodo is no *piccolo Cristo*, therefore, but a virtual Peter, betraying his most sacred obligation at the very last. Sam remarks that Frodo's failure was not utterly ruinous, for 'he was himself again, he was free'. Yet at first Frodo seems still under the delusion that he accomplished the high task himself, as he calls for them all to forgive Gollum: 'But for him, Sam, I could not have destroyed the Ring.' But then, far more truthfully, Frodo shifts from the active to the passive voice, acknowledging that he has been receptive no less than generative, as much acted upon as acting: 'For the Quest is achieved, and now all is over. I am glad you are here with me. Here at the end of all things, Sam.'¹¹

Such serene solemnity soon turns dour when the four returning hobbits discover that, during their year-long absence, Saruman and his henchmen, having won many of the hobbit-population to their side, have taken over the Shire. Their previously unspoiled realm has been atmospherically fouled with the pollution of smoking factories; politically oppressed by the installation of a bureaucratic regime;

and, not least of all, rendered utterly joyless by the shutting of the alehouses. Thus must the Shire first be scoured of its degradations before it can be truly reinhabited, as almost a hundred men and hobbits are left dead. When Sam and Frodo first approach Hobbiton itself, they cannot help marking the likeness of their once-blissful corner of Middle-earth to Sauron's savage realm: 'This is worse than Mordor!' says Sam. 'Much worse in a way. It comes home to you, as they say; because it is home, and you remember it before it was all ruined.'[12] Frodo's response is even more wrenching: 'The very last stroke [of the War against Sauron]. But to think that it should fall here, at the very door of Bag End! Among all my hopes and fears at least I never expected that.'[13] *Corruptio optima pessima* is a Latin tag that proves profoundly true: the ruin of the best is indeed the worst.

The final parting of Gandalf and Frodo from the other members of the Company as the two chief characters set sail from the Grey Havens cannot be mistaken as containing the eucatastrophic Joy that Tolkien hailed for being 'as poignant as grief'. It is indeed poignant but not with joy. It is filled, instead, with virtually unmitigated sadness. The struggle against Sauron and his evil forces has left Frodo too deeply wounded to live happily ever after. In fact, Frodo can't even return home again, as once more he resorts to the passive voice. 'I have been too deeply hurt, Sam. I tried to save the Shire, and it has been saved, but not for me. It must often be so, Sam, when things are in danger: some one has to give them up, lose them, so that others may keep them.'[14] So are Gandalf's final words similarly sorrowful: 'Well, here at last, dear friends, on the shores of the Sea comes the end of our fellowship in Middle-earth. Go in peace! I will not say: do not weep; for not all tears are an evil.'[15] Only the flint-hearted can witness the final departure of Gandalf and Frodo without turning misty-eyed. And while Sam is indeed the presumptive mayor-elect of Hobbiton, he returns with a muted kind of joy, as he draws a deep breath to make his exceedingly modest announcement. Not 'We won!' 'We destroyed the Ring!' 'We defeated Sauron!' but 'I'm back.'[16]

The fatalism of *The Children of Húrin*

An explanation for the melancholy quality of Tolkien's vision is to be found, I believe, in his celebrated essay on *Beowulf* entitled 'The Monsters and the Critics'. There he argues that this seventh- (perhaps ninth-) century Anglo-Saxon poem was written by an anonymous Christian, probably a monk, who poetically recorded the legend of Beowulf's long battle with Grendel – a struggle in which, while the monster is killed, so is Beowulf. This nameless Christian sought faithfully to preserve the brutality and grimness of the pagan life-world of the ancient Danish legend. Thus does he recount horrible battles and extol fierce loyalties, even as he shows that both men and events are overruled by the inexorable power of Fate, whose lowering clouds overshadow everything. The Venerable Bede, the English monk-historian who worked during this same period, records the witness of a converted Anglo-Saxon chieftain to the cheerlessness of pagan existence in the ancient North. This heathen leader likened life's brevity and fatality to a sparrow's flying into one end of a banquet-hall and out the other. Everything springs from cold black nothing-ness, it then enters into the brief moment of warmth and light called life, and it finally returns to the dark void whence it came. At the final battle of Ragnarök, the entire cosmos will be destroyed, and even the gods will die, as everything returns to 'Chaos and Unreason'.[17]

Tolkien also extols the nobility of these Nordic and Teutonic heroes in their 'doomed resistance' against inevitable defeat and death. The dragons of the deep against whom these manly warriors fought were made all the more ghastly because (as they believed) 'the evil spirits entered into the monsters and took visible shape in the hideous bodies'.[18] The heathen heroism of the Anglo-Saxons thus remains pertinent, Tolkien believed, not only to Darwinians haunted by the seemingly unguided randomness of the universe but also to Christians convinced of its ultimately providential order. Their 'creed of unyield-ing will', their 'absolute resistance, [made] perfect because without hope', their belief 'that man, each and all men, and all their works shall die', Tolkien argues, is 'a theme no Christian need despise'.[19]

From the myths and legends of the primeval North, Tolkien learned that no battle is finally won, no victory is ever complete – in this world at least – just as every triumph creates a host of new per-plexities. This perception on his part explains why it was that no sooner had he completed *The Lord of the Rings* than he returned to the ancient legends of Húrin and his doomed children, especially the gloomy tale of Túrin Turambar. My surmise is that Tolkien felt he had never done full justice to *wyrd* as it was understood by the

Anglo-Saxons. For *wyrd* is indeed a weird word. It's the Anglo-Saxon term usually rendered as 'fate', though its very pronunciation indicates something more than mere fatalism – the notion, namely, that things happen in eerie and unaccountable ways. *Wyrd* indicates the pagan view that the world is at least partially ruled by these supra-rational forces. Tolkien variously translates it to mean 'fate', 'doom', 'luck' or 'chance'. In every case, he seeks to remind his readers that our lives are governed by forces that we cannot control – even if they are finally governed by God.

Briefly put, *The Children of Húrin* concerns the curse of Morgoth. He has determined to demonstrate his monstrous sovereignty over all of Arda (earth) by destroying not only Húrin for having fought so wilfully against him but Húrin's innocent family as well:

> 'The shadow of my purpose lies upon Arda, and all that is in it bends slowly and surely to my will. But upon all whom you love my thought shall weigh as a cloud of Doom, and it shall bring them down into darkness and despair. Wherever they go, evil shall arise. Wherever they speak, their words shall bring ill counsel. Whatsoever they do shall turn against them. They shall die without hope, cursing both life and death.'[20]

On its face, such demonic *wyrd*-swearing seems to offer little promise. For if Húrin and his progeny are fated to bitter failure and death, why then follow their inevitably unhappy story? Tolkien doesn't help matters by adopting the distanced formality which he also used in *The Silmarillion*, with its rather stilted King James cadences and word inversions. Nor is the dense thicket of hard-to-pronounce personal and place names readily penetrated. The quality and character of the work's *dramatis personae* – as in the antique Northern epics that Tolkien so deeply admired – are revealed almost entirely by speech and action, so that we rarely find them making inward reflection on motives and purposes.

Even so, *The Children of Húrin* proves strangely fascinating. For while Tolkien abjured allegory, he approved of what he called 'applicability' – that is, the linking of things pre-historic and legendary with things historical and even contemporary, thus bringing his mythography into engagement with our own world. A little-noticed line in the first volume of *The Lord of the Rings* helps to make this connection. It contains an important key for unlocking this book that conveniently integrates the previously scattered episodes making up the life of Túrin Turambar. In *The Fellowship of the Ring*, the Company of Nine Walkers having found their path blocked by a huge snowstorm on Mount Caradhras, the wizard Gandalf cryptically declares that 'There are many evil and unfriendly things in the world that have little love for those that go on two legs, and yet are not in league with Sauron, but have purposes of their own. Some have been in this world longer than he.'[21]

As a thoroughly modern writer and believer, Tolkien seeks to acknowledge the reality of these 'evil and unfriendly things' and thus the abiding truth of *wyrd*: the presence of forces and powers that operate beyond the immediate (though not the ultimate) control of Ilúvatar, Tolkien's analogue to the sovereign God. After Darwin and Heisenberg, for example, it is hardly possible to deny the place of chance and accident, of hazard and uncertainty, amid what Tolkien calls 'the Circles of the World'. The Great Chain of Being – the Greek notion adopted by Christians that everything is ranged along a perfect continuum from inert minerals to fallen and unfallen angels, so that nothing happens by mere accident but everything with intrinsic purpose – this splendid chain of seamless continuity lies in pieces.

Despite all the later qualifications put on the breakthrough insights of Galileo and Newton in the seventeenth century, most of us still believe that (so far as we humans can discern) every natural effect is the product of its antecedent causes, *necessarily* so. Yet these natural occurrences seem not to be morally, much less mercifully, ordered. They appear to be prompted by material forces that collide and complement each other in often unpredictable ways, *chancily* so. To an extent heretofore unrecognized, we know that we are born with genetic predispositions, whether mental or physical, that set drastic limits on our prospects and possibilities. We are also the partial products, not only of environing influences, but also of just plain luck – of good or ill fortune, of *wyrd*. Who of us can say that we have chosen the true path at every turning, or that we have deserved every disaster that has befallen us, so that our lives can be entirely explained by the decisions we have rightly or wrongly made?

This is not for a trice to suggest that Tolkien regarded the universe as an unsponsored and undirected accident. On the contrary, it is Morgoth himself who is the absurdist and nihilist, here declaring that 'beyond the Circles of the World there is Nothing.'[22] Yet Tolkien seems to have questioned God's omnicausality as it is often conceived – namely, as if God were the divine Designer who, acting from beyond the universe, imposes his order from without. Tolkien appears to have sought, instead, a better way of affirming the providential order of the cosmos – namely, a means of acknowledging the weirdness of the world without attributing everything to the direct will of God. He seeks to discern how the non-coercive God wills the order of the world from within it, weaving its various causes and effects into a finally redemptive Whole. *The Children of Húrin* thus indicates that Ilúvatar works his will, not by directly manipulating these powers and forces, but rather by enabling a right human response to them. The web of things consists in a delicately spun tissue of interstitial and interdependent energies – most of them accidentally clashing and coinciding, many of them alien to immediate human benefit. Tolkien suggests that our lives can flourish, both morally and spiritually, only with a properly humbled acceptance of them. Even then we are guaranteed no happy outcome.

Húrin and his wife, Morwen, are deficient in this requisite humility, while their children Túrin and Niënor come to spurn it altogether. Yet the result is not outright and easily predicted disaster but rather a complex tangle of the good and the evil the outcome of which proves immensely sad, albeit only at the very end. Suffice it here to account only for Túrin's understandable and yet disastrous denial of *wyrd*. Because his father lies under the curse of Morgoth, Túrin's birth is accompanied by ill omens. The lines of his life are also straitened by his decidedly mixed, even contradictory, qualities: 'Túrin was slow to forget injustice or mockery . . . Yet he was quick to pity, and the hurts and sadness of living things might move him to tears . . .'[23] Thus while he proves to be a virtually invincible warrior, Túrin is also the product of what Tolkien's narrator calls 'unfriendly fortune': 'often what he designed went awry, and what he desired he did not gain; neither did he win friendship easily, for he was not merry, and laughed seldom, and a shadow lay on his youth'.[24]

As often proves true in Tolkien's work, his heroic characters are undone more by their virtues than their vices. Like Boromir in *The Lord of the Rings*, Túrin is so valiant in battle that he comes to think himself unconquerable. Yet why should he not, especially when his alliance with a brood of outlaws issues in good rather than evil things? Gradually, therefore, Túrin alters his name from Neithan the Wronged to Túrin Turambar ('Túrin the Master of Fate'). He thus refuses to heed the urging of his friend Beleg the elf-warrior not to make a direct assault on Morgoth's armies but rather to wait for the action of the Valar (the godlike creatures who have not broken faith with Ilúvatar) to rescue them. In his brusque refusal to trust Beleg, Túrin is described as 'being fey and unwitting of what lay before him'.[25] The antique word 'fey' is exceedingly ironic here, for it means 'fated' or 'doomed to death'. Rather than recognizing his own potential ruin at the hands of *wyrd*, Túrin begins to think himself a creature whose will and might are irresistible. In his incautious pride, therefore, Túrin mistakes Beleg for an orc and mistakenly slays him. Hence the wisdom of Gwindor, Túrin's companion in valour: 'The doom lies in yourself, not in your name.'[26]

Yet rather than moralizing over Túrin's vaulting hubris, Tolkien makes his self-doomed hero into a deeply sympathetic figure, more to be pitied than condemned. Like Oedipus and Siegfried and Beowulf, he comes to a dreadful end while accomplishing admirable deeds. In an act of unexampled valour, he slays the giant dragon Glaurung. Discontent even in his magnificent victory, Túrin labours riskily to draw his sword Gurthang from the Worm's belly. Yet again he oversteps, for no sooner has Túrin accomplished this daring deed than he learns that he has unwittingly married his own sister Niënor. The sword that he has mightily retrieved is useful only for piercing himself to death. Niënor in turn has committed similar self-slaughter upon learning that her husband is her brother.

Rather than leaving readers with the confident feeling that justice has been accomplished, however roughly, *The Children of Húrin* conveys the deep conviction that we too are ensnared in such unavoidable webs of guilt, so that none is innocent, not one. We also unwittingly commit vice, Tolkien reminds us, even in our virtuous acts. Mablung, one of the novel's noblest characters, is the immediate cause of Túrin's death for having told him the truth about his marriage. That truth-telling becomes the occasion for death-dealing is yet another example of the world's weirdness, for truth is meant to bring life and not death. Thus does Tolkien make Mablung's bitter lament also our own: 'I also have been meshed in the doom of the Children of Húrin, and thus with words have slain the one I loved.'[27]

Tolkien's sorrowful vision of joy

Yet this gloomy saying is the penultimate rather than the final word from Tolkien. Pagan greatness could not yet know that, under Christian aegis, the word *wyrd* would gradually come to connote not fate but providence. For while Sauron appears to control the Ring of addictive force until the very end, Tolkien hints that there is another and greater power working against it. We thus learn that Bilbo was *meant* to find the One Ring, even though he seemed to happen upon it by chance. The final triumph of the hobbits and the other 'weaklings' of Middle-earth over mighty Sauron and his demonic forces is enabled – discerning readers will notice – by an invisible sovereignty operating through them. Tolkien makes it occasionally visible, especially when, nearing the end of their wearying quest, Frodo and Sam are alone in Mordor. All their efforts seem finally to have failed. Even if somehow they succeed in destroying the Ring, there is no likelihood that they will survive, or that anyone will ever hear of their valiant deed. Even then, Sauron would take new form and wreak new ruin. Amid such apparent hopelessness, Sam – the bumbling and unreflective hobbit who has gradually emerged as a figure of moral and spiritual depth – beholds a single star shimmering above the dark clouds of Mordor:

> The beauty of it smote his heart, as he looked up out of the forsaken land, and hope returned to him. For like a shaft, clear and cold, the thought pierced him that in the end the Shadow was only a small and passing thing: there was light and high beauty for ever beyond its reach. . . . Now, for a moment, his own fate, and even his master's, ceased to trouble him. He crawled back into the brambles and laid himself by Frodo's side, and putting away all fear he cast himself into a deep untroubled sleep.[28]

Sam here discerns what our Northern ancestors could not yet perceive – namely, that light and shadow are not locked in dualistic combat; much less will the light finally be drowned in a sea of darkness, as at Ragnarök. However much the night may seem to triumph, it is the gleaming star that penetrates and defines the darkness.

This vision of ultimate joy and hope is a matter of action no less than of knowledge. Again, it is given to none other than Samwise Gamgee to discover the necessity not only of knowing but also of living according to the right Story. In the pass of Cirith Ungol, as he and Frodo have begun to doubt whether their Quest will ever succeed, Sam seeks to distinguish between enduring tales that matter and those that flare for a moment and then vanish. Many competing stories vie for human and hobbitic loyalty, and Sam is trying to locate their own narrative within the one hope-giving Story. He says to Frodo:

> '. . . we shouldn't be here at all, if we'd known more about it before we started. But I suppose it's often that way. The brave things in the old tales and songs, Mr Frodo: adventures, as I used to call them. I used to think that they were things the wonderful folk of the stories went out and looked for, because they wanted them, because they were exciting and life was a bit dull, a kind of a sport, as you might say. But that's not the way of it with the tales that really mattered, or the ones that stay in the mind. Folk seem to have been just landed in them, usually – their paths were laid that way, as you put it. But I expect they had lots of chances, like us, of turning back, only they didn't. And if they had, we shouldn't know, because they'd have been forgotten. We hear about those as just went on – and not all to a good end, mind you; at least not to what folk inside a story and not outside it call a good end. You know, coming home, and finding things all right, though not quite the same – like old Mr Bilbo. But those aren't always the best tales to hear, though they may be the best tales to get landed in! I wonder what sort of tale we've fallen into?'[29]

Sam has discerned the crucial divide. On the one hand, the tales that do not matter concern there-and-back-again adventures – escapades undertaken in search of excitement and in relief of boredom. The tales that rivet the mind, on the other hand, involve an unchosen Quest, a journey to which the pilgrims are strangely summoned. What counts, Sam adds, is not whether the Quest succeeds but whether the travellers turn back or slog ahead. One reason for not giving up, for not quitting, is that the great Sagas are told about those who refused to surrender – those who ventured forward in hope, even if to an uncertain finish. 'Don't the great tales never end?' Sam asks.[30] Frodo wisely answers in the negative. Yet their particular narrative, like those of other fellowships and companies, is sure to end. But if the wayfarers faithfully perform their minuscule roles in the grand cosmic Drama, others will advance the unfolding plot toward its final eucatastrophe. For this is the Story not of proud heroes striving mightily against evil, as in pagan epics, but of humble servants unwilling to kill fallen creatures who are ambiguously rather than absolutely evil. 'Things done and over and made into part of the great tales are different,' declares Sam. 'Why, even Gollum might be good in a tale.'[31]

It should be evident that Tolkien's vision is constituted by a complex interweaving of the pagan and the Christian, the despairing and the hopeful, the fated and the free. Yet these opposites are not set in endless dialectical play, as if first one and then the other gains the upper hand, nor as if they merge to produce some higher 'third' reality, in Hegelian fashion. On the contrary, Tolkien envisions them as integrated into a single vision of sorrowful joy. If these terms were reversed – into a joyful sorrow – then his vision would still be noble, but it would remain essentially tragic. Hence the rightful ordering of the sequence. Treebeard the Ent reflects on these matters after he has witnessed the orc-slaughter of his precious forest. Yet he finds solace in knowing that, even in defeat, 'we may help other peoples before we pass away'. Treebeard possesses what might well be called the essential Tolkienian demeanour, as the single most naive hobbit, the youthful Peregrin Took, has gained the wisdom to discern: 'Pippin could see a sad look in his eyes, sad but not unhappy.'[32] Treebeard is saddened at the thought of evil's sure victory within the bounds of time, but happier by far that he and his trustworthy trees can play their small but faithful part in the Drama wherein good can be temporarily but not finally defeated. It is a sorrowful joy indeed.

Notes

1 J. R. R. Tolkien, *The Letters of J. R. R. Tolkien*, ed. Humphrey Carter (Boston: Houghton Mifflin, 1981), p. 172.
2 Tolkien, *Letters*, pp. 172, 243.
3 J. R. R. Tolkien, *The Lord of the Rings* (Boston: Houghton Mifflin, 2001), p. 50.
4 Tolkien, *Letters*, p. 200.
5 Tolkien, *Lord of the Rings*, p. 356.
6 Tolkien, *Lord of the Rings*, p. 58.
7 Tolkien, *Lord of the Rings*, p. 924.
8 The rare book and manuscript librarians at Marquette University graciously allowed me to see these changes, inscribed in his own hand, that Tolkien made to the original typescript.

9 J. R. R. Tolkien, 'On Fairy-Stories', in *Essays Presented to Charles Williams*, ed C. S. Lewis (London: Oxford University Press, 1947), p. 81.
10 Tolkien, 'On Fairy-Stories', p. 84.
11 Tolkien, *Lord of the Rings*, p. 926.
12 Tolkien, *Lord of the Rings*, p. 994.
13 Tolkien, *Lord of the Rings*, p. 997.
14 Tolkien, *Lord of the Rings*, p. 1006.
15 Tolkien, *Lord of the Rings*, p. 1007.
16 Tolkien, *Lord of the Rings*, p. 1008.
17 J. R. R. Tolkien, *The Monsters and the Critics, and Other Essays*, ed. Christopher Tolkien (London: George Allen & Unwin, 1983), p. 21.
18 Tolkien, *Monsters and the Critics*, p. 22.
19 Tolkien, *Monsters and the Critics*, pp. 21, 23.
20 J. R. R. Tolkien, *The Children of Húrin*, ed. Christopher Tolkien (Boston: Houghton Mifflin, 2007), p. 64.
21 Tolkien, *Lord of the Rings*, p. 282.
22 Tolkien, *Children of Húrin*, p. 65.
23 Tolkien, *Children of Húrin*, p. 39.
24 Tolkien, *Children of Húrin*, pp. 81–2.
25 Tolkien, *Children of Húrin*, p. 119.
26 Tolkien, *Children of Húrin*, p. 170.
27 Tolkien, *Children of Húrin*, pp. 256–7.
28 Tolkien, *Lord of the Rings*, p. 901.
29 Tolkien, *Lord of the Rings*, p. 696.
30 Tolkien, *Lord of the Rings*, p. 697.
31 Tolkien, *Lord of the Rings*, p. 697.
32 Tolkien, *Lord of the Rings*, p. 475.

Bibliography

1 References

Auden, W. H. *For the Time Being: A Christmas Oratorio*. In *Collected Longer Poems*, pp. 131–97. New York: Random House, 1969.

Babington Smith, Constance. Introduction. In *Last Letters to a Friend, 1952– 1958*, by Rose Macaulay, pp. 13–25. New York: Atheneum, 1963.

———. Introduction. In *Letters to a Friend, 1950–1952*, by Rose Macaulay, pp. 11–23. New York: Atheneum, 1962.

———. *Rose Macaulay*. London: Collins, 1972.

Baillie, John. *Our Knowledge of God*. London: Oxford University Press, 1939.

Barfield, Owen. 'C. S. Lewis'. 1964. In *Owen Barfield on C. S. Lewis*, edited by G. B. Tennyson, pp. 3–16. Middletown, CT: Wesleyan University Press, 1989.

———. 'Lewis, Truth and Imagination'. 1978. In *Owen Barfield on C. S. Lewis*, edited by G. B. Tennyson, pp. 90–103. Middletown, CT: Wesleyan University Press, 1989.

———. *Poetic Diction: A Study in Meaning*. London: Faber and Gwyer, 1928.

Bensen, Alice R. *Rose Macaulay*. New York: Twayne, 1969.

Betjeman, John. Introduction. In *Godly Mayfair*, edited by Ann Callender, pp. iv–v. London: Grosvenor Chapel, 1980.

Brown, David. *Discipleship and Imagination: Christian Tradition and Truth*. Oxford: Oxford University Press, 2004.

———. *God and Mystery in Words: Experience through Metaphor and Drama*. Oxford: Oxford University Press, 2008.

———. *Tradition and Imagination: Revelation and Change*. Oxford: Oxford University Press, 2004.

Brown, Peter. *Augustine of Hippo: A Biography*. Berkeley: University of California Press, 1967.

Carnell, Corbin Scott. 'Imagination'. In *The C. S. Lewis Readers' Encyclopedia*, edited by Jeffrey D. Schultz and John G. West, pp. 214–15. Grand Rapids, MI: Zondervan, 1998.

Carpenter, Humphrey. *The Inklings: C. S. Lewis, J. R. R. Tolkien, Charles Williams and Their Friends*. 1978. Reprint, London: HarperCollins, 2006.

Crawford, Alice. *Paradise Pursued: The Novels of Rose Macaulay*. Madison: Fairleigh Dickinson University Press, 1995.

Curtis, Philip. *A Hawk Among Sparrows: A Biography of Austin Farrer.* London: SPCK, 1985.

Dante Alighieri. *Paradise,* translated by Dorothy L. Sayers and Barbara Reynolds. Harmondsworth: Penguin, 1962.

Eliot, T. S. Introduction. In *All Hallows' Eve,* by Charles Williams, pp. ix–xviii. New York: Pellegrini & Cudahy, 1948.

Emery, Jane. *Rose Macaulay: A Writer's Life.* London: John Murray, 1991.

Farrer, Austin. 'Can Myth Be Fact?' In *Interpretation and Belief,* edited by Charles C. Conti, pp. 165–75. London: SPCK, 1976.

———. *The Crown of the Year: Weekly Paragraphs for the Holy Sacrament.* London: Dacre, 1952.

———. 'Emptying Out the Sense'. In *Austin Farrer: The Essential Sermons,* edited by Leslie Houlden, pp. 117–20. London: SPCK, 1991.

———. *Faith and Speculation.* New York: New York University Press, 1967.

———. *Finite and Infinite: A Philosophical Essay.* 1943. 2nd edn, London: Dacre, 1959.

———. *The Glass of Vision.* London: Dacre, 1948.

———. 'Keble and His College'. In *The End of Man,* edited by Charles C. Conti, pp. 153–7. London: SPCK, 1973.

———. 'The Prior Actuality of God'. 1966. In *Reflective Faith,* edited by Charles C. Conti, pp. 178–91. London: SPCK, 1972.

———. 'Prologue: On Credulity'. In *Interpretation and Belief,* edited by Charles C. Conti, pp. 1–6. London: SPCK, 1976.

———. *A Rebirth of Images: The Making of St John's Apocalypse.* London: Dacre, 1949.

———. *Saving Belief: A Discussion of Essentials.* 1964. Reprint, Harrisburg, PA: Morehouse, 1994.

———. *The Triple Victory: Christ's Temptations According to St Matthew.* London: Faith, 1965.

———. 'A University Sermon'. 1948. In *A Hawk Among Sparrows: A Biography of Austin Farrer,* by Philip Curtis, pp. 232–39. London: SPCK, 1985.

———. 'Very God and Very Man'. 1952. In *Interpretation and Belief,* edited by Charles C. Conti, pp. 126–37. London: SPCK, 1976.

Francis, Mark R. 'Sacramental Theology'. In *The Blackwell Encyclopedia of Modern Christian Thought,* edited by Alister E. McGrath, pp. 581–7. Oxford: Blackwell, 1995.

Fromm, Gloria G. 'The Worldly and Unworldly Fortunes of Rose Macaulay'. *The New Criterion* 5, no. 2 (1986), pp. 38–44.

Greer, Rowan A. *Broken Lights and Mended Lives: Theology and Common Life in the Early Church.* University Park: Pennsylvania State University Press, 1986.

Gresham, William Lindsay. Preface. In *The Greater Trumps*, by Charles Williams, pp. i–x. New York: Pellegrini & Cudahy, 1950.

Harned, David Baily. *Faith and Virtue*. Philadelphia: United Church Press, 1973.

———. *Images for Self-Recognition: The Christian as Player, Sufferer and Vandal*. New York: Seabury, 1977.

Hein, David. 'A Note on C. S. Lewis's *The Screwtape Letters*'. *The Anglican Digest* 49, no. 2 (2007), pp. 55–8.

Lawrence, D. H. *Studies in Classic American Literature*. 1923. Reprint, New York: Viking, 1961.

Lewis, C. S. 'Bluspels and Flalansferes: A Semantic Nightmare'. 1939. In *Selected Literary Essays*, edited by Walter Hooper, pp. 251–65. Cambridge: Cambridge University Press, 1969.

———. *Broadcast Talks*. London: Geoffrey Bles, 1942.

———. *The Collected Letters of C. S. Lewis*, edited by Walter Hooper. 3 vols. [San Francisco]: HarperSanFrancisco, 2004–7.

———. *An Experiment in Criticism*. Cambridge: Cambridge University Press, 1961.

———. *The Four Loves*. London: Geoffrey Bles, 1960.

———. *The Great Divorce*. London: Geoffrey Bles, 1945.

———. 'The Language of Religion'. In *Christian Reflections*, edited by Walter Hooper, pp. 129–41. Grand Rapids, MI: Eerdmans, 1967.

———. *Letters to Malcolm: Chiefly on Prayer*. New York: Harcourt, Brace & World, 1963.

———. 'Man or Rabbit?' 1946[?]. In *God in the Dock: Essays on Theology and Ethics*, edited by Walter Hooper, pp. 108–13. Grand Rapids, MI: Eerdmans, 1970.

———. *Mere Christianity*. London: Geoffrey Bles, 1952.

———. 'Myth Became Fact'. 1944. In *God in the Dock: Essays on Theology and Ethics*, edited by Walter Hooper, pp. 63–7. Grand Rapids, MI: Eerdmans, 1970.

———. Preface. In *Essays Presented to Charles Williams*, edited by C. S. Lewis, pp. v–xiv. London: Oxford University Press, 1947.

———. *The Problem of Pain*. London: Centenary, 1940.

———. 'Reason'. In *Poems*, edited by Walter Hooper, p. 81. London: Geoffrey Bles, 1964.

———. 'Religion: Reality or Substitute?' 1941. In *Christian Reflections*, edited by Walter Hooper, pp. 37–43. Grand Rapids, MI: Eerdmans, 1967.

———. *Surprised by Joy: The Shape of My Early Life*. New York: Harcourt, Brace and World, 1955.

Loades, Ann. 'The Sacramentalist's Agenda'. In *Feminist Theology: Voices from the Past*, pp. 167–92. Cambridge: Polity; Malden, MA: Blackwell, 2001.

Lobdell, Jared, ed. *The Detective Fiction Reviews of Charles Williams, 1930–1935*. Jefferson, NC, and London: McFarland, 2003.

Macaulay, Rose. *Last Letters to a Friend, 1952–1958*, edited by Constance Babington Smith. New York: Atheneum, 1963.

———. *Letters to a Friend, 1950–1952*, edited by Constance Babington Smith. New York: Atheneum, 1962.

———. *Letters to a Sister*, edited by Constance Babington Smith. New York: Atheneum, 1964.

———. *Personal Pleasures*. New York: Macmillan, 1936.

———. *The Towers of Trebizond*. 1956. Reprint, New York: New York Review Books, 2003.

———. *The World My Wilderness*. 1950. Reprint, London: Virago, 1983.

Moore, Judith. 'Rose Macaulay: A Model for Christian Feminists'. *Christian Century* 95 (1978), pp. 1098–1101.

Neufeldt, Victoria, ed. *Webster's New World College Dictionary*. 3rd edn. New York: Macmillan, 1996.

Reynolds, Barbara. 'Take Away the Camel, and All Is Revealed'. *Church Times*, 8 September 2000, pp. 14–15.

Richards, I. A. *Principles of Literary Criticism*. London: Kegan Paul, 1925.

Sayers, Dorothy L. *Begin Here: A Statement of Faith*. New York: Harcourt, Brace, 1941.

———. *Busman's Honeymoon*. 1937. Reprint, London: New English Library, 1977.

———. *Child and Woman of Her Time*. Vol. 5 of *The Letters of Dorothy L. Sayers*, edited by Barbara Reynolds. Cambridge: Dorothy L. Sayers Society, 2002.

———. *Creed or Chaos?* New York: Harcourt, Brace, 1949.

———. 'Dante and Charles Williams'. In *The Whimsical Christian*, pp. 180–204. New York: Macmillan, 1978.

———. *Gaudy Night*. 1935. Reprint, London: New English Library, 1970.

———. *The Greatest Drama Ever Staged*. London: Hodder and Stoughton, 1938.

———. 'Hymn in Contemplation of a Sudden Death'. In Dorothy L. Sayers, *Spiritual Writings*, selected and introduced by Ann Loades, pp. 10–11. London: SPCK, 1993.

———. *The Just Vengeance*. London: Victor Gollancz, 1946.

———. *The Mind of the Maker*. 1941. Reprint, San Francisco: Harper-SanFrancisco, 1987.

———. *The Nine Tailors*. 1934. Reprint, London: New English Library, 1982.

———. *The Poetry of Dorothy L. Sayers*, edited by Ralph E. Hone. Cambridge: Dorothy L. Sayers Society in association with the Marion E. Wade Center, 1996.

————. *Unpopular Opinions*. London: Victor Gollancz, 1946.

Schakel, Peter J. *Imagination and the Arts in C. S. Lewis: Journeying to Narnia and Other Worlds*. Columbia: University of Missouri Press, 2002.

————. *Reason and Imagination in C. S. Lewis: A Study of 'Till We Have Faces'*. Grand Rapids, MI: Eerdmans, 1984.

Shideler, Mary McDermott. *The Theology of Romantic Love: A Study in the Writings of Charles Williams*. New York: Harper, 1962.

Sidney, Philip. *Sir Philip Sidney's Defense of Poesy*, edited by Lewis Soens. Lincoln: University of Nebraska Press, 1970.

Starr, Charlie W. 'Meaning, Meanings, and Epistemology in C. S. Lewis'. *Mythlore* 25, no. 3/4 (Spring/Summer 2007), pp. 161–82.

Thorson, Stephen. 'Barfield's Evolution of Consciousness: How Much Did Lewis Accept?' *Seven: An Anglo-American Literary Review* 15 (1998), pp. 9–35.

————. 'Knowing and Being in C. S. Lewis's "Great War" with Owen Barfield'. *The Bulletin of the New York C. S. Lewis Society* 15, no. 1 (November 1983), pp. 1–8.

————. '"Knowledge" in C. S. Lewis's Post-Conversion Thought: His Epistemological Method'. *Seven: An Anglo-American Literary Review* 9 (1988), pp. 91–116.

————. 'Lewis and Barfield on Imagination'. Part 1, *Mythlore* 17, no. 2 (Winter 1990), pp. 12–18, 32; Part 2, *Mythlore* 17, no. 3 (Spring 1991), pp. 16–21.

Tolkien, J. R. R. *The Children of Húrin*, edited by Christopher Tolkien. Boston: Houghton Mifflin, 2007.

————. *The Letters of J. R. R. Tolkien*, edited by Humphrey Carpenter. Boston: Houghton Mifflin, 1981.

————. *The Lord of the Rings*. 1954, 1955. Reprint, Boston: Houghton Mifflin, 2001.

————. *The Monsters and the Critics, and Other Essays*, edited by Christopher Tolkien. London: George Allen & Unwin, 1983.

————. 'On Fairy-Stories'. In *Essays Presented to Charles Williams*, edited by C. S. Lewis, pp. 38–89. London: Oxford University Press, 1947.

Urang, Gunnar. *Shadows of Heaven: Religion and Fantasy in the Writing of C. S. Lewis, Charles Williams, and J. R. R. Tolkien*. Philadelphia: Pilgrim, 1971.

Webster, Harvey Curtis. *After the Trauma: Representative British Novelists since 1920*. Lexington: University Press of Kentucky, 1970.

Williams, Charles. *All Hallows' Eve*. 1945. Reprint, Vancouver, BC: Regent College Publishing, 2002.

————. 'Blake and Wordsworth'. In *The Image of the City, and Other Essays*, edited by Anne Ridler, pp. 59–67. London: Oxford University Press, 1958.

———. *Charles Williams: Essential Writings in Theology and Spirituality*, edited by Charles Hefling. Cambridge, MA: Cowley, 1993.

———. 'The Church Looks Forward'. In *The Image of the City*, pp. 154–8 (as 'The Way of Affirmation'); in *Charles Williams: Essential Writings*, pp. 139–45.

———. 'The Cross'. In *The Image of the City*, pp. 131–9; in *Charles Williams: Essential Writings*, pp. 191–203.

———. *Descent into Hell*. 1937. Reprint, Grand Rapids, MI: Eerdmans, 1999.

———. *The Descent of the Dove: A Short History of the Holy Spirit in the Church*. 1939. Reprint, Grand Rapids, MI: Eerdmans, 1968.

———. *The Figure of Beatrice*. 1943. Reprint, Berkeley: Apocryphile, 2005.

———. *The Greater Trumps*. 1932. Reprint, New York: Pellegrini & Cudahy, 1950.

———. *He Came Down from Heaven/The Forgiveness of Sins*. London: Faber and Faber, 1950.

——— 'The Image of the City in English Verse'. In *The Image of the City*, pp. 92–102.

———. 'Natural Goodness'. In *The Image of the City*, pp. 75–80; in *Charles Williams: Essential Writings*, pp. 35–41.

———. *Outlines of Romantic Theology*, edited by Mary Alice Hadfield. Grand Rapids, MI: Eerdmans, 1990.

———. 'The Productions of Time'. *Time and Tide* 22 (25 January 1941), pp. 72–3.

———. 'The Redeemed City'. In *The Image of the City*, pp. 102–10; in *Charles Williams: Essential Writings*, pp. 151–63.

———. 'St John'. In *The Image of the City*, pp. 87–9; in *Charles Williams: Essential Writings*, pp. 61–3.

———. *Taliessin through Logres, The Region of the Summer Stars, and Arthurian Torso*. Grand Rapids, MI: Eerdmans, 1974.

Williams, Donald T. 'Christian Poetics, Past and Present'. In *The Christian Imagination*, edited by Leland Ryken, pp. 3–21. Rev. edn. Colorado Springs: Shaw Books, 2002.

Williams, Rowan. *Anglican Identities*. Cambridge, MA: Cowley, 2003.

2 Further Reading

Adey, Lionel. *C. S. Lewis's 'Great War' with Owen Barfield*. Victoria, BC: English Literary Studies, University of Victoria, 1978.

Allen, Diogenes. 'Faith and the Recognition of God's Activity'. In *Divine Action: Essays Inspired by Austin Farrer's Philosophical Theology*, edited by Brian Hebblethwaite and Edward Henderson, pp. 197–210. Edinburgh: T. & T. Clark, 1990.

Bibliography

Auden, W. H. 'Charles Williams'. *Christian Century* 73 (2 May 1956), pp. 552–4.

Bassham, Gregory. 'Lewis and Tolkien on the Power of the Imagination'. In *C. S. Lewis as Philosopher: Truth, Goodness and Beauty*, edited by David Baggett, Gary R. Habermas and Jerry L. Walls, pp. 245–60. Downers Grove, IL: InterVarsity, 2008.

Bigger, Charles. *Between Chora and the Good: Metaphor's Metaphysical Neighborhood*. New York: Fordham University Press, 2005.

———. 'Models and Maps'. *Southern Journal of Philosophy* 1 (1963), pp. 8–13.

Brabazon, James. *Dorothy L. Sayers*. New York: Scribner's, 1981.

Bray, Suzanne, and Richard Sturch, eds. *Charles Williams and His Contemporaries*. Newcastle upon Tyne: Cambridge Scholars Publishing, 2009.

Brown, David. 'The Role of Images in Theological Reflection'. In *The Human Person in God's World: Studies to Commemorate the Austin Farrer Centenary*, edited by Brian Hebblethwaite and Douglas Hedley, pp. 85–105. London: SCM, 2006.

Cavaliero, Glen. *Charles Williams: Poet of Theology*. Grand Rapids, MI: Eerdmans, 1983.

Como, James T., ed. *C. S. Lewis at the Breakfast Table, and Other Reminiscences*. 1979. Reprint, New York: Harcourt, Brace, 1992.

Conti, Charles. *Metaphysical Personalism: An Analysis of Austin Farrer's Metaphysics of Theism*. Oxford: Clarendon, 1995.

Dale, Alzina Stone. *Maker and Craftsman: The Story of Dorothy L. Sayers*. Wheaton, IL: Harold Shaw, 1992.

Downing, Chrystal. *Writing Performances: The Stages of Dorothy L. Sayers*. London: Palgrave Macmillan, 2004.

Eaton, Jeffrey C., and Ann Loades, eds. *For God and Clarity: New Essays in Honor of Austin Farrer*. Allison Park, PA: Pickwick, 1983.

Farrer, Austin. 'An English Appreciation'. In *Kerygma and Myth: A Theological Debate*, edited by H. W. Bartsch, pp. 212–23. New York: Harper, 1972.

Foster, Robert. *The Complete Guide to Middle-earth*. New York, Ballantine, 1974.

Hadfield, Mary Alice. *Charles Williams: An Exploration of His Life and Work*. New York: Oxford University Press, 1983.

Harned, David Baily. *Patience: How We Wait Upon the World*. Cambridge, MA: Cowley, 1997.

Hebblethwaite, Brian, and Edward Henderson, eds. *Divine Action: Essays Inspired by the Philosophical Theology of Austin Farrer*. Edinburgh: T. & T. Clark, 1990.

Hedley, Douglas. 'Austin Farrer's Shaping Spirit of Imagination'. In *The Human Person in God's World: Studies to Commemorate the Austin Farrer*

Centenary, edited by Brian Hebblethwaite and Douglas Hedley, pp. 106–34. London: SCM, 2006.

———. *Living Forms of the Imagination*. London and New York: T. & T. Clark/ Continuum, 2008.

Hefling, Charles. *Jacob's Ladder: Theology and Spirituality in the Thought of Austin Farrer*. Cambridge, MA: Cowley, 1979.

Hein, David. 'Austin Farrer on Justification and Sanctification'. *The Anglican Digest* 49, no. 1 (2007), pp. 51–4.

———. 'Faith and Doubt in Rose Macaulay's *The Towers of Trebizond*'. *Anglican Theological Review* 88 (2006), pp. 47–68.

———. 'Farrer on Friendship, Sainthood, and the Will of God'. In *Captured by the Crucified: The Practical Theology of Austin Farrer*, edited by David Hein and Edward Hugh Henderson, pp. 119–48. New York and London: T. & T. Clark/Continuum, 2004.

———. 'Hugh Lister (1901–44): Priest, Labor Leader, Combatant Officer'. *Anglican and Episcopal History* 70 (2001), pp. 353–74.

———. 'Saints: Holy, Not Tame'. *Sewanee Theological Review* 49 (2006), pp. 204–17.

Hein, David, and Edward Hugh Henderson, eds. *Captured by the Crucified: The Practical Theology of Austin Farrer*. New York and London: T. & T. Clark/Continuum, 2004.

Hein, David, and Charles R. Henery, eds. *Spiritual Counsel in the Anglican Tradition*. Cambridge: James Clarke, 2010.

Henderson, Edward Hugh. 'The Divine Playwright'. *Personalist Forum* 12 (1996), pp. 35–80.

———. 'Double Agency and the Relation of Persons to God'. In *The Human Person in God's World: Studies to Commemorate the Austin Farrer Centenary*, edited by Brian Hebblethwaite and Douglas Hedley, pp. 38–64. London: SCM, 2006.

———. 'Homo Symbolicus'. *Man and World* 12 (1971), pp. 131–50.

———. 'Incarnation and Double Agency'. In *Truth, Religious Dialogue and Dynamic Orthodoxy: Reflections on the Works of Brian Hebblethwaite*, edited by Julius Lipner, pp. 154–64. London: SCM, 2005.

Hone, Ralph E. *Dorothy L. Sayers: A Literary Biography*. Kent: Kent State University Press, 1979.

Hooper, Walter. 'Oxford's Bonny Fighter'. In *C. S. Lewis at the Breakfast Table, and Other Reminiscences*, edited by James T. Como, pp. 137–85. New York: Macmillan, 1979.

Howard, Thomas. *The Novels of Charles Williams*. New York: Oxford University Press, 1983.

Huttar, Charles A. 'A Lifelong Love Affair with Language: C. S. Lewis's Poetry'. In *Word and Story in C. S. Lewis*, edited by Peter J. Schakel and

Charles A. Huttar, pp. 86–108. Columbia: University of Missouri Press, 1991.

Huttar, Charles A., and Peter J. Schakel, eds. *The Rhetoric of Vision: Essays on Charles Williams.* Lewisburg, PA: Bucknell University Press; London: Associated University Presses, 1996.

Kenney, Catherine. *The Remarkable Case of Dorothy L. Sayers.* Kent: Kent State University Press, 1990.

Lewis, C. S. 'Tolkien's *The Lord of the Rings*'. In *On Stories, and Other Essays on Literature,* edited by Walter Hooper, pp. 83–90. New York: Harcourt Brace Jovanovich, 1982.

Lewis, C. S., ed. *Essays Presented to Charles Williams.* London: Oxford University Press, 1947.

Lloyd, Genevieve. *The Man of Reason: 'Male' and 'Female' in Western Philosophy.* London: Routledge, 1993.

Loades, Ann. *Feminist Theology: Voices from the Past.* Cambridge: Polity; Malden, MA: Blackwell, 2001.

Loades, Ann, and Michael McLain, eds. *Hermeneutics, the Bible and Literary Criticism.* New York: St Martin's, 1992.

MacSwain, Robert C. 'A Fertile Friendship: C. S. Lewis and Austin Farrer'. *The Chronicle of the Oxford University C. S. Lewis Society* 5, no. 2 (May 2008), pp. 22–45.

———. 'Solved by Sacrifice: Austin Farrer, Fideism and the Evidence of Faith'. PhD dissertation, University of St Andrews, 2010.

MacSwain, Robert C. and Michael Ward, eds. *The Cambridge Companion to C. S. Lewis.* Cambridge: Cambridge University Press, 2010. Manzo, Bernard. 'The Test of Literature: John Henry Newman's holy imaginings'. *Times Literary Supplement,* 30 July 2010, 14–15.

Medcalf, Stephen. 'The Coincidence of Myth and Fact'. In *The Spirit of England: Selected Essays of Stephen Medcalf,* edited by Brian Cummings and Gabriel Josipovici, pp. 20–40. London: Modern Humanities Research Association and Maney Publishing, 2010.

Pearce, Joseph. *Tolkien: Man and Myth.* San Francisco: Ignatius, 1998.

Reynolds, Barbara. *Dorothy L. Sayers: Her Life and Soul.* New York: St Martin's, 1993.

Ridler, Anne. Introduction. In *The Image of the City, and Other Essays,* by Charles Williams, pp. ix–lxxii. 1958. Reprint, Berkeley: Apocryphile, 2007.

Rutledge, Fleming. *The Battle for Middle-earth: Tolkien's Divine Design in 'The Lord of the Rings'.* Grand Rapids, MI, and Cambridge, UK: Eerdmans, 2004.

Sayers, Dorothy L. *Are Women Human?* 1947, 1971. Reprint, Grand Rapids, MI, and Cambridge, UK: Eerdmans, 2005.

_____. *The Christ of the Creeds, and Other Broadcast Messages to the British People during World War II*, introduced by Suzanne Bray. Hurstpierpoint: Dorothy L. Sayers Society, 2008.

_____. *The Poetry of Dorothy L. Sayers*, edited by Ralph E. Hone. Cambridge: Dorothy L. Sayers Society in association with the Marion E. Wade Center, 1996.

_____. *Spiritual Writings*, selected and introduced by Ann Loades. London: SPCK, 1993.

Sayers, Dorothy L., and Jill Paton Walsh. *Thrones, Dominations*. London: Hodder and Stoughton, 1998.

Schakel, Peter J. *The Way into Narnia: A Reader's Guide*. Grand Rapids, MI: Eerdmans, 2005.

Shideler, Mary McDermott. *The Theology of Romantic Love: A Study in the Writings of Charles Williams*. New York: Harper, 1962.

Shippey, Tom. *The Road to Middle-earth*. Boston: Houghton Mifflin, 2003.

Sibley, Agnes. *Charles Williams*. Boston: Twayne, 1982.

Simmons, Laura K. *Creed Without Chaos: Exploring Theology in the Writings of Dorothy L. Sayers*. Grand Rapids, MI: Baker, 2005.

Slocum, Robert Boak. *Light in a Burning-Glass: A Systematic Presentation of Austin Farrer's Theology*. Columbia: University of South Carolina Press, 2007.

Tolkien, J. R. R. *The Silmarillion*, edited by Christopher Tolkien. London: HarperCollins, 1994.

Walsh, Jill Paton, and Dorothy L. Sayers. *A Presumption of Death*. London: Hodder and Stoughton, 2002.

Ward, Benedicta. *Anselm of Canterbury: His Life and Legacy*. London: SPCK, 2009.

Ward, Michael. *Planet Narnia: The Seven Heavens in the Imagination of C. S. Lewis*. New York: Oxford University Press, 2008.

Williams, Charles. *The Figure of Beatrice: A Study in Dante*. 1943. Reprint, Woodbridge: Boydell & Brewer, 1994.

Wood, Ralph C. *The Gospel According to Tolkien: Visions of the Kingdom in Middle-earth*. Louisville, KY: Westminster John Knox, 2003.

Index

Index